Frommer's®

P O R T A B L E

New Orleans

1st Edition

by Lisa M. Legarde

Macmillan • USA

ABOUT THE AUTHOR

Lisa M. Legarde was born in New Orleans and still has wonderful childhood memories of Mardi Gras and artists "on the fence" at Jackson Square. She loves Cajun food and music and is passionate about jazz.

MACMILLAN TRAVEL

A Simon & Schuster Macmillan Company
1633 Broadway
New York, NY 10019
Find us online at **http://www.mgr.com/travel** or
on America Online at Keyword: **Frommer's**

ISBN 0-02-861423-2
ISSN 1090-316X

Material in this guide is excerpted from *Frommer's New Orleans '97*.
Map Editor: Douglas Stallings
Design by Michele Laseau
Digital Cartography by John Decamillas and Ortelius Design
Maps copyright ©, by Simon & Schuster, Inc.

SPECIAL SALES

Bulk purchases (10+ copies) of Frommer's and selected Macmillan travel guides are available to corporations, organizations, mail-order catalogs, institutions, and charities at special discounts, and can be customized to suit individual needs. For more information write to Special Sales, Macmillan General Reference, 1633 Broadway, New York, NY 10019.

Manufactured in the United States of America

Contents

List of Maps

AN INVITATION TO THE READER

In researching this book, we discovered many wonderful places. We're sure you'll find others. Please tell us about them, so we can share the information with your fellow travelers in upcoming editions. If you were disappointed with a recommendation, we'd love to know that, too. Please write to:

Lisa M. Legarde
Frommer's Portable New Orleans, 1st Edition
Macmillan Travel
1633 Broadway
New York, NY 10019

AN ADDITIONAL NOTE

Please be advised that travel information is subject to change at any time, and this is especially true of prices. We therefore suggest that you write or call ahead for confirmation when making your travel plans. The authors, editors, and publisher cannot be held responsible for the experiences of readers while traveling. Your safety is important to us, however, so we encourage you to stay alert and be aware of your surroundings. Keep a close eye on cameras, purses, and wallets, all favorite targets of thieves and pickpockets.

WHAT THE SYMBOLS MEAN

✪ Frommer's Favorites
Hotels, restaurants, attractions, and entertainment you should not miss.

⑤ Super-Special Values
Hotels and restaurants that offer great value for the money.

The following abbreviations are used for credit cards:

AE	American Express	EU	Eurocard
CB	Carte Blanche	JCB	Japan Credit Bank
DC	Diners Club	MC	MasterCard
DISC	Discover	V	Visa
ER	enRoute		

Planning a Trip to New Orleans

*T*his chapter contains all the nuts-and-bolts information you'll need to plan your trip to New Orleans. Everything is at your fingertips, from where to get visitor information to which airlines fly into town.

1 Visitor Information & Money

VISITOR INFORMATION

I would advise even the most seasoned traveler to write or call ahead to the **New Orleans Metropolitan Convention and Visitors Bureau,** at 1520 Sugar Bowl Dr., New Orleans, LA 70112 (☎ **504/566-5055**), for their brochures and information about the city. They're extremely friendly and helpful, and you can easily get any information you can't find in this book from them. Another source of information is the **Greater New Orleans Black Tourism Network** (☎ **504/523-5652**).

MONEY

High season rates are in effect through any of the major festivals (see Chapter 2), as well as at other times throughout the spring. New Orleans is also quite popular in the fall. Summer months are the least expensive, mainly because the heat and humidity make traveling at this time less appealing.

Many travelers still prefer to carry traveler's checks for security, but it's becoming easier all the time to access your ATM network on the road. Your bank at home might have a list of ATM locations that will accept your card. Some centrally located ATMs in New Orleans are First National Bank of Commerce (240 Royal St.), Hibernia National Bank (701 Poydras St.), and Whitney National Bank (228 St. Charles Ave.).

2   When to Go

CLIMATE

The average temperature in New Orleans is 70°F, but the thermometer can drop or rise considerably in a single day. The high humidity can make relatively mild temperatures feel uncomfortably cold or uncomfortably warm. The city's climate will be pleasant almost any time of year except July and August, which can be exceptionally muggy. If you do come during those months, you'll quickly learn to follow the natives' example and stay out of the noonday sun and duck from one air-conditioned building to another. And even in the rain (an average of 63 inches falls annually), you'll be able to get around without difficulty, mainly because it comes in great downpours that don't last too long.

If you're coming to New Orleans in the dead of summer, T-shirts and shorts are absolutely acceptable (except in the city's finest restaurants). In the spring and fall, something a little warmer is in order; in the winter, you'll probably need a lightweight coat or jacket.

New Orleans's Average Temperatures & Rainfall

	Jan	Feb	Mar	Apr	May	June	July	Aug	Sept	Oct	Nov	Dec
High (°F)	56	58	62	69	76	81	83	83	79	71	61	57
High (°C)	13	14	16	19	23	25	26	26	24	20	15	14
Rainfall	10	9	9	7	8	10	15	13	10	5	7	10

NEW ORLEANS CALENDAR OF EVENTS

For more information on the major New Orleans events, see Chapter 2.

January

- **The USF&G Sugar Bowl Classic.** This is New Orleans's oldest yearly sporting event (it originated in 1934). The football game is the main event, but there are also tennis, swimming, basketball, sailing, running, and flag-football competitions. New Year's Day.

February

- **Lundi Gras celebrations.** This free, annual outdoor event at Spanish Plaza features fireworks, a parade, and a masked ball. For details, contact New Orleans Riverwalk (☎ **504/522-1555**). Monday before Mardi Gras Day.

- ✪ **Mardi Gras.** The culmination of the two-month-long Carnival season, Mardi Gras is the annual blow-out that New Orleans is famous for. The entire city stops working and starts partying early in the morning.

Where: All over the city something will be happening. The great parades go through the Central Business District instead of the French Quarter. **When:** For 1997 the date is February 11. **How:** Contact the New Orleans Metropolitan Convention and Visitors Bureau (☎ **504/566-5055**).

March

- **Black Heritage Festival.** This celebration honors the African Americans who have made, and are making, great cultural contributions to New Orleans. Contact the Black Heritage Foundation (☎ **504/827-0112**) for more information.

- **St. Patrick's Day Parades.** There are two of them; one takes place in the French Quarter beginning at Molly's at the Market (1107 Decatur St.), and the other goes through the Irish Channel neighborhood following a parade route that begins at Race and Annunciation streets and ends at Jackson Street. For information on the French Quarter parade call **504/525-5169**; for the Irish Channel parade call **504/565-7080.**

- **Tennessee Williams New Orleans Literary Festival.** This four-day event includes theatrical performances, readings, discussion panels, master classes, musical events, and literary walking tours dedicated to the playwright. Call the University of New Orleans, Metro College Conference Services (☎ **504/286-6680**). Late March.

- ✪ **Spring Fiesta.** The fiesta, which begins with the crowning of the Spring Fiesta queen, is more than half a century old. Some of the city's historic private homes, courtyards, and plantation homes are opened for special tours.

    Where: Locations throughout the city. **When:** Late March to early April. **How:** For a current schedule, call Spring Fiesta (☎ **504/581-1367**).

April

- ✪ **The French Quarter Festival.** This is a relatively new event, just over a decade old, that celebrates New Orleans's history. It's kicked off with a parade down Bourbon Street, and, among other things, you can join people dancing in the streets, learn the history of jazz, visit historic homes, and take a ride on a riverboat.

    Where: All over the French Quarter. **When:** Mid-April. **How:** Call French Quarter Festivals, Inc. (☎ **504/596-5730**).

✪ **The New Orleans Jazz and Heritage Festival.** Jazz Fest is so popular that the city tends to sell out its lodging, sometimes up to a year in advance. Thousands of musicians, cooks, and craftspeople come together to strut their stuff. If you like jazz, Cajun, zydeco, or New Orleans rhythm and blues with that shuffling, "second-line" rhythm, don't miss the event.

   Where: Fair Grounds Race Track and various venues throughout the city. **When:** Usually the last weekend in April and the first weekend in May. **How:** Call Jazz Fest (☎ **504/522-4786**).

• **The Crescent City Classic.** This 10,000-meter road race, sponsored by the *Times-Picayune* and Coca-Cola, brings an international field of top runners to the city. It begins at Jackson Square and ends at Audubon Park. For more information, call **504/861-8686.**

May

• **Greek Festival.** This annual three-day event at the Hellenic Cultural Center features Greek folk dancing, specialty foods, crafts, and music. For more information, call the Holy Trinity Cathedral (☎ **504/282-0259**).

June

• **The Great French Market Tomato Festival.** A two-day celebration of the diversity of the tomato, with cooking and tastings in the historic French Market. For more information call **504/522-2621.**

• **Reggae Riddums Festival.** A gathering of calypso, reggae, and soca musicians is held annually in City Park. It's a three-day extravaganza with both ethnic foods and arts and crafts. For more information call **504/367-1313** or 800/367-1317.

July

• **Go Fourth on the River.** New Orleans's annual July 4th celebration. Events begin in the morning at the New Orleans river-front and continue into the night, culminating in a spectacular fireworks display. For more information call (☎ **504/528-9994**).

• **New Orleans Wine and Food Experience.** Wine and food tastings are held in antique shops and art galleries throughout the French Quarter. Seminars by wine makers and local chefs, vintner dinners, and grand tastings are also offered. More than 150 wines and 40 restaurants are featured every day. For information call **504/529-9463.** Late July.

August

- **African Heritage Festival International.** This three-day event celebrates the culture and music of the local African-American community. There's food, dance, arts and crafts, and activities for the kids. For more information call the African Heritage Foundation (☎ 504/949-5610).

October

- **Art for Arts' Sake.** The season begins with gallery openings throughout the city. Julia, Magazine, and Royal streets are where the action is. For more information, contact the Contemporary Arts Center (☎ 504/523-1216).
- **Swamp Festival.** Sponsored by the Audubon Institute, the Swamp Festival features hands-on contact with Louisiana swamp animals. Admission to the festival is free with zoo admission. For information, call the Audubon Institute (☎ 504/861-2537). Over two weekends at the end of September and the beginning of October.
- **Louisiana Jazz Awareness Month.** Nightly concerts (some of which are free), television and radio specials, and lectures, all sponsored by the Louisiana Jazz Foundation. For more information and a schedule of events call the Louisiana Jazz Federation at **504/522-3154.**
- **Gumbo Festival**. In a city that loves its food, this festival showcases one of the city's favorites. There are a number of events that highlight Cajun culture, and the entertainment is continuous. The Gumbo Fest is held in Bridge City. For information, contact the Gumbo Festival (☎ 504/436-4712).
- **New Orleans Film and Video Festival.** New Orleans's film festival is a relatively young event. Canal Place Cinemas and other theaters throughout the city screen award-winning local and international films and host writers and directors. The event lasts one week. Admission prices range from $3 to $12. Call **504/523-3818** for 1997 dates.
- ✪ **Halloween.** Spectacular costumes and memorable people-watching in the French Quarter. Events include Boo-at-the-Zoo (October 30 and 31) for children, a number of costume parties (including a Monster Bash at the Ernest N. Morial Convention center), the Anne Rice Vampire Lestat Extravaganza, and the Moonlight Witches Run.

Where: All over the city, but the French Quarter, as always, is the center of action. **When:** October 31. **How:** Contact the New Orleans Metropolitan Convention and Visitors Bureau (☎ **504/566-5055**).

December

- **A New Orleans Christmas.** Throughout December, there's candlelight caroling in Jackson Square, and the old New Orleans homes get dressed up especially for the occasion. Restaurants offer multicourse Réveillon dinners and hotels throughout the city offer "Papa Noel" rates. For information, contact French Quarter Festivals (☎ **504/522-5730**).
- **New Year's Eve.** The countdown to 1998 will take place in Jackson Square (one of the country's biggest street parties). Revelers watch a lighted ball—à la New York City—as it drops from the top of Jackson Brewery.

3 Getting There

BY PLANE

The Major Airlines No fewer than 13 airlines fly to New Orleans's Moisant International Airport; among them are **American Airlines** (☎ **800/433-7300**); **Continental Airlines** (☎ **800/ 525-0280** or 504/581-2965); **Delta Airlines** (☎ **800/221-1212**); **Northwest Airlines** (☎ **800/225-2525**); **Southwest Airlines** (☎ **800/435-9792**); and **TWA** (☎ **504/529-2585**).

New Orleans International Airport The airport is located 15 miles west of the city in Kenner. You'll find information booths scattered around the airport and in the baggage claim area, and a branch of the **Travelers Aid Society** (☎ **504/464-3522**) is also here.

From the airport you can reach the Central Business District by bus for $1.10. The bus leaves the airport and goes to the downtown side of Tulane Avenue between Elks Place and South Saratoga Street every 12 to 15 minutes from 6 to 9am and from 3 to 6pm, every 23 minutes at other times. Buses run from 6am to 6:30pm. For information call **504/737-9611.**

You can also get to your hotel by **Airport Shuttle** (☎ **504/ 522-3500**). The ride will cost $10 per person (one way), and the van will take you directly to your hotel. There are airport shuttle information desks (staffed 24 hours) in the airport. *Note:* If you plan to take the airport shuttle back to the airport when you depart, you must call a day in advance and let them know what time your flight is leaving. They will then tell you what time they will pick you up.

A taxi from the airport will cost you $21; if there are three or more passengers, the fare will be $8 per person.

If you want to ride in style from the airport to your hotel, contact **Olde Quarter Livery** (☎ **504/595-5010**). Express transfer service from New Orleans International Airport is available at a rate of $50 for a four-passenger stretch limousine and $65 for a six-passenger limousine. You'll be greeted by a uniformed chauffeur and escorted to the car, which will be waiting just outside the airport's baggage claim area. Drivers are prompt and efficient—you'll never be left waiting.

BY CAR

You can drive to New Orleans via I-10, U.S. 90, and U.S. 61, and across the Lake Pontchartrain Causeway on La. 25.

It's a good idea to call before you leave home to ask for directions to your hotel. Most hotels have parking facilities (for a fee); if they don't, they'll give you the names and addresses of nearby parking lots.

AAA (☎ **800/926-4222**) will assist members with trip planning, service aids, and emergency services.

Renting a Car   All major national car rental companies are represented at the airport, including **Alamo** (☎ **800/327-9633**); **Avis** (☎ **800/331-1212**); **Budget** (☎ **800/527-0700**); **Dollar** (☎ **800/800-4000**); **Hertz** (☎ **800/654-3131**); and **National** (☎ **800/227-7368**). See "Getting Around" in Chapter 4 for more information on car rental and driving in New Orleans.

BY TRAIN

Amtrak trains reach New Orleans's Union Passenger Terminal, 1001 Loyola Ave. (☎ **800/USA-RAIL** or 504/524-7571 for Amtrak information and schedules), from Los Angeles and intermediate points; New York, Washington, and points in between; and Chicago and intermediate points. Using the All Aboard America fares, you'll pay $188 to $208 from New York or Chicago, and $248 to $288 from Los Angeles. Amtrak frequently offers senior-citizen discounts and other packages, some with a rental car, so be sure to check when you reserve.

Amtrak also does an especially good job with tour packages, which can be arranged through your local Amtrak Tour Desk.

Options might range from a ticket with hotel accommodations to an air/rail package—take the train and then fly back to your destination, or choose from eight other combinations of tour packages. Prices will change, of course, during the life of this book, but from past experience it is safe to say that Amtrak tours will be genuine money-savers.

The train station is located in the Central Business District, and there will be plenty of taxis outside the main entrance of the passenger terminal. It will be a short ride to your hotel if you're staying in the French Quarter or the Central Business District.

2

Mardi Gras & Other Festivals

*N*ew Orleans means "festival"—if you don't believe it, try this simple little free-association test. What's the first thing that comes to mind when someone says "New Orleans"? Mardi Gras, right? Well, that's the biggie, of course, but it's only one of this lively city's celebrations. There's something about the frame of mind here that just won't tolerate inhibitions—whether there's a declared celebration in progress or not.

As for officially designated festival days, a calendar of events issued by the New Orleans Metropolitan Convention and Visitors Bureau lists no fewer than 26 spread over the year that are observed either in the city proper or in its neighboring parishes. There's a festival of jazz and food; a celebration of spring, when women don the costumes of long ago and shepherd the public through gorgeous old mansions; numerous food festivals that celebrate the fine art of eating as it's practiced around here; and, well, you get the idea. If there's any possible reason to celebrate, New Orleans throws a party.

I can't, of course, cover them all in these pages. I'll tell you about some of the most interesting, and you can find others listed in the "Calendar of Events" in Chapter 1. You should also contact the **New Orleans Metropolitan Convention and Visitors Bureau,** 1520 Sugar Bowl Dr., New Orleans, LA 70112 (☎ **504/566-5055**), to see what else might be happening when you visit. If, however, you don't see anything spectacular listed for the dates of your trip, don't worry—New Orleans is the kind of city that makes you feel festive from the moment you arrive.

1 Mardi Gras

Mardi Gras, the mother of all New Orleans parties, has been here in one form or another as long as the city itself. Volumes could be written about its history, and almost any native you encounter will have his or her own store of Mardi Gras tales. What follows here is a quick rundown on present-day krewes, parades, and balls.

To begin with, the name *Mardi Gras* means "Fat Tuesday" in French, and that's a very appropriate name because it is always celebrated on the Tuesday before Ash Wednesday—the idea being that you have an obligation to eat, drink, and be as merry as you possibly can before the 40-day Lenten season of fasting and repentance sets in. The name *Carnival* is Latin in origin (from *carnisvale,* meaning "farewell to flesh") and refers to the six- to eight-week stretch from Twelfth Night, or January 6, to Mardi Gras Day. In New Orleans, the Carnival season is officially opened by the Krewe of Twelfth Night Revelers ball, the only ball that has a fixed date.

WHAT TO SEE & DO

What can you expect to see and take part in if you come to New Orleans for Mardi Gras? First, you must remember that this is, primarily, a party New Orleans throws for itself—those spectacular balls are private, attended only by members and their invited guests. Attendance is by invitation, not by ticket, except, that is, for the Bacchus supper dance (and even those tickets are usually hard to come by). If you should be invited to a krewe ball, there are a few things you should know. You'll be a spectator, not a participant, and unless you're a woman and have been issued a "call-out" card, you'll be seated in a separate section to view the tableau after the previous year's queen and her court have been escorted to seats of honor and masked-and-costumed krewe members have taken their reserved, up-front seats. Members, who guard their secrecy not just during Mardi Gras but year-round, are always in costumes and masks—for men it's white tie and tails if the invitation reads *de rigueur,* tuxedos if it reads only *formal.* Women, of course, are always in ball gowns. Those lucky "call-out" women will be seated separately from other guests (even their escorts) until the dancing begins and they've been called out by the krewe member who sent them the card. After a turn around the floor, they'll be given a krewe favor (a souvenir representative of that year's ball theme) and returned to their escorts. As members of the krewe and their ladies continue dancing, the current "royal court" will repair to the queen's supper, where friends and guests will be entertained the rest of the night—and into the morning.

One of the nicest things about New Orleans's private party is that the whole world is invited to come and look, and there are a whole slew of not-so-private entertainments. If you think this town's restaurants and nightclubs and bars and jazz clubs are pretty special most of the time, you should see them during Carnival! You can, in fact, form your own informal "krewe" of friends and have a ball that might be as much fun as those private ones, just by making the rounds in a group.

Whatever else you do or don't do, you surely won't miss seeing a Mardi Gras parade—if, that is, you come during the final 11 days of Carnival. You'll know one's coming when you hear the scream of motorcycle sirens and a herd of motorized police come into view. They'll be followed by men on horseback (sometimes mounted police, sometimes krewe members) who clear the edges of the streets for the approaching floats. The king's float is first in line, with his majesty enthroned and waving to the mass of cheering humanity with his scepter. Then will come a float with a banner proclaiming the theme of the parade. After that, each float will illustrate some facet of the theme. And it's a grand sight—the papier-mâché lions or elephants or flowers or fanciful creatures or whatever are sometimes enormous (there are people in New Orleans who work all year designing and building Mardi Gras floats), and there's much use of silver and gold tinsel that sparkles in the sunlight or the light of torches. Those torches, or flambeaux, are carried by costumed dancers. Each float has masked krewe members who wave and throw doubloons and souvenirs. In some of the parades, the floats keep coming until you think there's no end to them—in one recent year, Bacchus had 23 and Rex had 25. Each krewe has its designated time and parade route (which makes a current Mardi Gras guidebook invaluable) and most follow some part of St. Charles Avenue, sometimes a portion of Jackson Street as well, and Canal Street, and end up at the Municipal Auditorium, where all parades disband—except the renegade Bacchus, which has a Rivergate terminus. Because there are more than 50 parading krewes and only 11 days in which to do the parading, the streets are seldom empty, day or night, during this period. And the rollicking, costumed crowd filling the streets is as much something to see as the parades themselves. Every conceivable manner of costume appears, and maskers made bold by their temporary anonymity carry on in the most outrageous, hilarious manner imaginable. A great good humor envelops the whole scene.

On Mardi Gras, the last day of Carnival, the walking clubs are out at the crack of dawn, King Zulu arrives around 9am, the Rex parade is midmorning, and Comus closes the day with its evening parade (about 6:30pm). The high point of the final day is probably when Rex, the only Mardi Gras king whose identity is disclosed, arrives on his majestic float. It is a very high honor to be chosen Rex, and the selection always comes from among prominent men in the city,

Some Mardi Gras Tips

Catching a Throw   If someone throws you something from a float or a balcony and it actually makes it to the ground, don't go after it with your hands—step on it first to let everyone around you know that it's yours. When interest in what's under your foot wanes it's safe to pocket the treasure. Otherwise, you'll probably end up with several broken fingers.

Parking   Parking in New Orleans during Mardi Gras can be both costly and next to impossible, so you're best off to leave your car at the hotel and walk or take a cab to your intended spot along the parade route. Parking along the parade route is not allowed two hours before and two hours after the parade. In addition, although you'll see people leaving their cars on "neutral ground" (the median in the street), it is illegal to park there and the chances are good that you'll be towed. Parking and driving around the French Quarter are also restricted. If your hotel is in the French Quarter you can probably get a pass that will allow you access to your hotel's parking area.

Liquor Laws   Liquor laws in New Orleans are quite lax. Many bars are open 24 hours during Mardi Gras, and drinking is allowed on the street. However, for safety reasons, you are required to have drinks in plastic "geaux" (or "go") cups.

Crime   Not surprisingly, the streets of New Orleans are a haven for pickpockets during Mardi Gras. Take precautions.

most well past the first blush of youth. Rex's queen, on the other hand, is always one of the current year's pack of debutantes. Although they make for a pretty ill-matched royal couple, there've never been any reports of incompatibility between the rulers-for-a-day. The choosing of Rex and his queen is done in the strictest secrecy, adding to the excitement that attends their first public appearance in the parade.

PLANNING YOUR FESTIVAL

Now for the practicalities. First, you can't really just drop in. If you do, you may find yourself sleeping in Jackson Square or on a sidewalk somewhere. Accommodations are booked solid in the city itself and in the nearby suburbs, *so make your plans well ahead and book a room as soon as the plans are finalized.* It is no exaggeration to say that you should make your plans a full year or more in advance. Prices are usually higher during Mardi Gras, and most hotels and guest houses impose minimum-stay requirements.

If you want to join the maskers in costume it's best to plan ahead and come prepared; there are, however, several shops in town that specialize in Mardi Gras costumes and masks (see Chapter 7). One of the most reasonable is the **Mardi Gras Center,** 831 Chartres St. (☎ **504/524-4384**). If you come early enough they can custom-make a costume to your specifications; if not, they are well stocked with new and used costumes, wigs, masks, hats, and makeup.

When you arrive, remember that while the huge crowds add to the general merriment, they also make it more difficult to get in and out of restaurants in a hurry. And your progress from one part of town to another will be slowed down considerably. So be sure to come in a relaxed frame of mind and with enough mental flexibility for the delays to be a source of enjoyment and not irritation— after all, who knows what you may see while waiting.

You'll enjoy Mardi Gras more, too, if you've done a little homework before your trip. Contact the **New Orleans Metropolitan Convention and Visitors Bureau,** 1520 Sugar Bowl Dr., New Orleans, LA 70112 (☎ **504/566-5055**), and ask for their current Mardi Gras information.

CAJUN MARDI GRAS

For a really unique Mardi Gras experience, drive out to Cajun Country. Lafayette, a booming but charming town in the very heart of French Acadiana, celebrates Carnival in a manner quite different from New Orleans's fete—a manner that reflects the Cajun heritage and spirit. There are three full days of activities leading up to Mardi Gras that are designed to *laissez les bons temps rouler* ("let the good times roll"—an absolute creed around these parts during Carnival). This is, in fact, second in size only to New Orleans's celebration, and there's one *big* difference—the Cajuns open their final pageant and ball to the general public. That's right, you can don your formal wear and join right in.

Instead of Rex and his queen, the Lafayette festivities are ruled by King Gabriel and Queen Evangeline. They are the fictional hero and heroine of Longfellow's epic poem *Evangeline*, which was based on real-life lovers who were separated during the British expulsion of Acadians from Nova Scotia just after the French and Indian War, and their story is still very much alive here among the descendants of those who shared their wanderings. Things get off to a joyous start

Mardi Gras from 1997 to 2000

You can always figure out the date of Mardi Gras because it falls exactly 46 days before Easter. If you can't find your calendar, or just can't be bothered with the math, the following will help:

1997	February 11
1998	February 24
1999	February 16
2000	March 7

with the Children's Krewe and Krewe of Bonaparte parades and ball the Saturday before Mardi Gras, following a full day of celebration at Acadian Village. On Monday night Queen Evangeline is honored at the Queen's Parade. The King's Parade, held the following morning, honors King Gabriel and opens a full day of merriment. Lafayette's African-American community stages the Parade of King Toussaint L'Ouverture and Queen Suzanne Simonne about noon, just after the King's Parade. And following that, the Krewe of Lafayette invites everyone to get into the act as its parade winds through the streets. Krewe participants trot along on foot or ride in the vehicle of their choice—some very imaginative modes of transportation turn up every year. The Mardi Gras climax, a brilliantly beautiful, exciting formal ball presided over by the king and queen and their royal court, takes place that night. Everything stops promptly at midnight, as Cajuns and visitors alike depart to observe the solemnity of Lent with the fondly remembered glow of Mardi Gras to take them through to Easter.

Out in the Cajun countryside that surrounds Lafayette, there's yet another form of Mardi Gras celebration, and I'll guarantee you won't find another like it anywhere else in the world. It's very much tied to the rural lifestyle of these displaced people who have created a rich culture out of personal disaster. And since Cajuns firmly believe that nothing is ever quite as much fun alone as it is when shared, you're entirely welcome to come along. The rural celebration goes like this: Bands of masked men dressed in patchwork costumes and peaked hats (*capichons*) set off on Mardi Gras morning on horseback, led by their *capitaine*. They ride from farm to farm, asking at each, "Will you receive the Mardi Gras?" (*"Voulez-vous reçevoir le Mardi Gras?"*) and dismounting as the invariable "Yes" comes in reply. Then each farmyard becomes a miniature festival, as the revelers "make monkeyshines" (*faire le macaque*) with song and dance, much drinking of beer, and other antics loosely labeled as "entertainment." As payment for their show, they demand, and get, "a fat little chicken to make a big gumbo."

When each band has visited its allotted farmyards, all the bands head back to town, where everyone else has already begun the general festivities. There'll be dancing in the streets, rowdy card games, storytelling, and the like until the wee hours, and you may be sure that all those "fat little chickens" go into the "gumbo gros" pot to make a "big gumbo." It's a really "down home" sort of festival. And if you've never heard Cajun music or eaten gumbo cooked by real Cajuns, you're in for a treat.

You can write or call ahead for full particulars on both these Mardi Gras celebrations. Contact **Lafayette Parish Convention and Visitors Commission,** P.O. Box 52066, Lafayette, LA 70505 (☎ **800/346-1958** in the United States, 318/232-3808, or 800/ 543-5340 in Canada).

2 New Orleans Jazz & Heritage Festival

By the time mid-April rolls around, Easter has passed, the Mardi Gras is a fond memory of this year and a grand expectation for next, and New Orleanians turn to another festival celebration: the New Orleans Jazz and Heritage Festival (Jazz Fest). The festival began 26 years ago, when producer George Wein (who founded the Newport Jazz Festival, among others) organized a concert involving 300 musicians. It was held in Congo Square and included artists such as Duke Ellington, Al Hirt, Pete Fountain, and Mahalia Jackson. The festival got off to a slow start, with only about 150 people in the audience, but it has grown over the years into what has become known as one of this country's greatest music festivals.

The Jazz and Heritage Festival actually combines two fetes, as its name implies. From one weekend to another (usually the last weekend in April and the first weekend in May), musicians, mimes, artists, craftspeople, and chefs head out to the Fairgrounds Race Track on the weekends and settle into hotel ballrooms, jazz joints, concert halls, and a special evening concert site to put on a never-ending show of what New Orleans is all about. More than 4,000 performers turn up—and that's not counting the street bands. Famous-name jazz, rock, pop, R&B, Cajun, zydeco, Latin, ragtime, Afro-Caribbean, folk, rap, country, bluegrass, and gospel musicians are drawn to this festival, and they very happily share 11 stages out at the fairgrounds with lesser-known and local groups. Some of the big-name artists who attended last year's festival were Dr. John, Bela Fleck and the Flecktones, Allen Toussaint, Indigo Girls, Buckwheat Zydeco, the Neville Brothers, Joan Osborne, Phish, the Dave Matthews Band, The Radiators, Wynton Marsalis, Van Morrison, and Joan Baez. You can find your favorites and stand in front of the stage all day long or make the rounds and come back to see which new group has taken the stage. Remember that this is a New Orleans festival—completely unstructured with the emphasis on pure enjoyment.

If this sounds like a lot of entertainment, keep in mind that this is only what's happening out at the fairgrounds; on weeknights, street bands are everywhere, and if you can't find a performance of your kind of music going on somewhere, it must not exist. And if traditional jazz happens to be your preference, you'll be in heaven.

As for the "heritage" part of the festival, local craftspeople and imported artisans arrive at Jazz Fest en masse with their wares. Demonstrations are offered throughout the festival. You might get to see Louisiana Native American basket making; Cajun accordion, fiddle, and triangle making; decoy carving; boat building; and Mardi Gras Indian beading and costume making. Contemporary arts and crafts, like jewelry, furniture, hand-blown glass, and paintings, are also featured. At Congo Square you'll find an open marketplace filled with contemporary and traditional African (and African-influenced) crafts and performing artists. Additionally, delicious food is available from about 50 booths: Red beans and rice, jambalaya, gumbo, crawfish, sweet-potato pie, oysters, fried chicken, andouille, boudin, po-boys, crabs, and shrimp are always featured. You can also get Caribbean, African, Spanish, Italian, and soul food. And, there's plenty of cold beer available to wash everything down. There's just nothing quite like munching fried chicken from the Second Mount Triumph Missionary Baptist Church booth in an outdoor setting where the air is filled with strains of traditional jazz, ragtime, reggae, and the blues.

To find out about the current dates, the artists who will be there, and where they'll be performing in concert during the week, contact the **New Orleans Jazz and Heritage Festival,** 2000 Royal St., New Orleans, LA 70177 (☎ **504/522-4786**). Tickets, which should be purchased as early as February, are available through TicketMaster. To inquire about mail orders call **504/522-5555.** To order tickets by phone, or to get ticket information, call **800/ 488-5252** outside Louisiana or 504/522-5555. To order by fax dial

504/379-3291. Tickets for the festival cost $10 in advance and $15 at the gate for adults, and $1.50 in advance and $2 at the gate for children. Evening events and concerts (tickets should be ordered in advance for these events as well) may be attended at an additional cost (usually between $17.50 and $30, depending on the concert).

A word about Jazz Fest parking and transportation: Basically, it's next to impossible to park at the fairgrounds. There are a small number of places available at a cost of $10 a day; however, I don't know anyone who has ever been lucky enough to get a space there (certainly not for the entire weekend). I strongly recommend that you take public transportation or one of the available shuttles. The Regional Transit Authority operates bus routes from various pickup points to the fairgrounds. For schedules and information call **504/248-3900.** Taxis, though probably scarce, will also take you to the fairgrounds at a special event rate of $3 per person (or the meter reading if it is higher). I recommend **United Cabs** (☎ **504/ 524-9606**). The New Orleans Jazz and Heritage Festival will provide information about shuttle transportation, which is usually available at an additional cost to the ticket price.

Note: If you're flying to New Orleans specifically for the Jazz and Heritage Festival, consider calling **Continental Airlines** (☎ **800/ 525-0280**). They're the official airline for the Jazz and Heritage Festival and they offer special fares during the event. Before you call Continental, call the festival's information line and ask for the Jazz Fest promotional code.

3 Other Festivals

SPRING FIESTA

One of the best times of the year to visit New Orleans is during the five-day-long Spring Fiesta, which has been going on since 1935. This is one time you can get to see the inside of some of those lovely old homes ordinarily closed to the public. Hostesses clad in antebellum dress will escort you through the premises and provide all sorts of information and anecdotes about these homes and historic buildings. In the French Quarter, there are balcony concerts by sopranos rendering numbers sung there in the past by Jenny Lind and Adelina Patti. Out on River Road, there are plantation home tours; and as a highlight there is the gala "Night in Old New Orleans" parade, which features carriages bearing passengers dressed as prominent figures in the city's history and some of the best marching bands in town.

Spring Fiesta usually takes place during one week in April. For full details, reservations, and a schedule of the admission fees (around $15 for City Tours, $45 for Country Estate Tours) for some of the homes, contact **Spring Fiesta Association,** 826 St. Ann St., New Orleans, LA 70116 (☎ 504/581-1367). You can order tickets by mail, or you can purchase tickets at the French Market Gift Shop, 824 Decatur St., as well as at Gray Line Tour Desks. For a list of locations, contact the Spring Fiesta Association.

TENNESSEE WILLIAMS FESTIVAL

In late March or early April, New Orleans honors one of its most illustrious writers. Tennessee Williams, although not born here, once said, "If I can be considered to have a home, it would have to be New Orleans . . . which has provided me with more material than any other city." During the three-day Tennessee Williams/New Orleans Literary Festival, many of his plays are performed, and there are symposiums and panel discussions on his work, as well as walking tours of his favorite French Quarter haunts. For dates and details, contact the **University of New Orleans,** Metro College Conference Services ED 122, New Orleans, LA 70148 (☎ **504/ 286-6680**).

FRENCH QUARTER FESTIVAL

The three-day French Quarter Festival in early April (from April 11 to April 13 in 1997) is a spectacular conglomeration of all the ingredients of the unique French Quarter's rich gumbo of life. There are scores of free outdoor concerts, patio tours, a parade, a battle of jazz bands, art shows, children's activities, and talent and bartender competitions. As if that weren't enough, Jackson Square is transformed into the world's largest jazz brunch, when about 40 leading restaurants turn out to serve Cajun/Creole specialties such as jambalaya, gumbo, and crawfish fettucine. For exact dates and other information, write to **French Quarter Festivals,** 100 Conti St., New Orleans, LA 70130 (☎ 504/522-5730).

CREOLE CHRISTMAS

Trust New Orleans! A few days simply are not enough for this lively city to celebrate Christmas, so the entire month of December is designated "Creole Christmas." There are all sorts of gala events sprinkled throughout the month's calendar, including tours of 19th-century homes decorated for the holiday, candlelight caroling in Jackson Square, cooking demonstrations, a madrigal dinner, gingerbread house demonstrations, and special Réveillon menus at select

French Quarter restaurants (including Arnaud's, Begue's, the Rib Room, and Alex Patouts). Special "Papa Noël" rates are offered by hotels citywide from December 5 to December 25. For full details, contact **French Quarter Festival,** 100 Conti St., New Orleans, LA 70130 (☎ **504/522-5730**).

FESTIVALS ACADIENS

This is a Cajun Country celebration—or rather, six celebrations—held during the third week of September in Lafayette. These festivals, lumped under the heading Festivals Acadiens, pay tribute to the culture and heritage of Cajun families who have been here since the British expelled them from their Nova Scotia homeland 200 years ago. The festive week includes the Bayou Food Festival, the Festival de Musique Acadienne, the Louisiana Native Crafts Festival, the Acadiana Fair and Trade Show, the RSVP Senior Fair and Craft Show, and Downtown Alive.

At the **Bayou Food Festival,** you'll be able to taste the cuisine of more than 30 top Cajun restaurants. Specialties such as stuffed crabs, crawfish étouffée, oysters Bienville, shrimp Creole, oysters Rockefeller, shrimp de la Teche, catfish en brochette, jambalaya, chicken-and-sausage gumbo, smothered quail, and hot boudin are everyday eating for Cajuns, and this is a rare opportunity to try them all. The Bayou Food Festival is held in Girard Park adjacent to the music festival. Admission is free.

The Festival de Musique Acadienne began in 1974 when some Cajun musicians were engaged to play briefly for visiting French newspaper editors. It was a rainy night, but some 12,000 Cajun residents showed up to listen. The walls rang for three solid hours with old French songs, waltzes, two-steps, Cajun rock rhythms, zydeco, and the special music some have dubbed "Cajun Country." Since then it has become an annual affair, with more than 50,000 visitors usually on hand. Because of the crowds, the festival is now held outdoors in Girard Park, where fans can listen in grassy comfort. Performed almost entirely in French, the music includes both traditional and modern Cajun styles, including zydeco (a form that combines the blues with more traditional Cajun sounds). The music starts early and ends late, and there's no charge to come to the park and listen. All money from sales of food and beverage stands goes to fund public service projects of the Lafayette Jaycees.

You'll see native Louisiana artisans demonstrating their skills at the **Louisiana Native Crafts Festival.** All crafts must have been practiced before or during the early 1900s, and all materials used must be native to Louisiana. Meeting these criteria are such arts as woodcarving of all types (with an emphasis, it seemed to me, on duck decoys), soap making, pirogue making (pronounced *PEE-rogue*—it's a Cajun canoe, one variety of which is made from a dugout cypress log) chair caning, doll making, palmetto weaving, Native American–style basket weaving, quilting, spinning, dyeing, pottery making, jewelry making, and alligator skinning.

The **Acadiana Fair and Trade Show** is put on by Lafayette merchants and businesspeople, and there's an indoor display of their goods and services, plus an outdoor carnival with rides, a midway, and games. It's sponsored by the Lafayette Jaycees, and free shuttle bus service for the public from one festival to another is provided by the city.

The elders who have passed crafts down to many of the younger Cajuns you'll see at the Native Crafts Festival have their day in the sun at the **RSVP Senior Fair and Craft Show** (the RSVP stands for Retired Senior Volunteer Program). They're all over 60, and it's a rare treat to meet them and see their homemade articles and listen to them talk of the old days.

You can visit the **Acadian Village** any time of the year, but during Festivals Acadiens, special events are often scheduled. If you have any interest at all in Acadiana's history, you'll find this little village an interesting trip back in time. Homes and buildings here are not models or reconstructions—they're all original old Acadian homes that have been restored and moved to the village to create (or, as the Cajuns say, "reassemble") a typical 1800s village. It's a tranquil, charming spot.

For exact dates and full details on Festivals Acadiens, write or call the **Lafayette Parish Convention and Visitors Commission,** P.O. Box 52066, Lafayette, LA 70505 (☎ **800/346-1958** in the United States, 318/232-3808, or 800/543-5340 in Canada).

RAYNE FROG FESTIVAL

To prove my point that just about anything is cause for celebration in New Orleans and its environs, let me tell you about the **Rayne Frog Festival.** It's held in Cajun Country, just a few miles west of Lafayette. The Cajuns can hold their own when it comes to drumming up festivals—a harvest, a new season, a special tradition, or just the job of being alive—and in this case they simply turn to the lowly frog as an excuse for a *fais-dodo* (dance) and a waltz contest. Not to forget the reason for it all, things get underway with frog races and frog-jumping contests—and if you arrive without your frog, there's a "Rent-a-Frog" service. To wind things up, there's a lively frog-eating contest. The Rayne Frog Festival is held in September. For dates and full details, contact the **Lafayette Parish Convention and Visitors Commission,** P.O. Box 52066, Lafayette, LA 70505 (☎ **800/346-1958** in the United States, 318/232-3808, or 800/543-5340 in Canada).

3

Getting to Know New Orleans

*N*ew Orleans is a small city, so you'll have no problem getting your bearings and finding your way around. The people are extraordinarily helpful and friendly, but if you still need some help, you'll find listed below just about everything you need to know.

1 Orientation

VISITOR INFORMATION

You'll be way ahead if, as far in advance as possible, you contact the **New Orleans Metropolitan Convention and Visitors Bureau,** 1520 Sugar Bowl Dr., New Orleans, LA 70112 (☎ **504/ 566-5005**), for their brochures on sightseeing, dining, entertainment, and shopping. The Convention and Visitors Bureau can also be reached by e-mail at tourism@nawlins.com. If you have a special interest, they'll help you plan your visit around appropriate activities. The internet address for the Convention and Visitors Bureau is http://www.nawlins.com. Other internet addresses worth checking out are http://www.nola.com and http://www.neworleans.net. From those addresses you'll also be able to access other New Orleans–specific sites.

Once you've arrived, you can stop by the **Visitor Information Center** at 529 St. Ann St. (☎ **504/566-5031**), in the French Quarter. The center is open daily from 9am to 5pm and has excellent walking- and driving-tour maps and booklets on restaurants, accommodations, sightseeing, special tours, and almost anything else you might want to know about. The staff is friendly and knowledgeable about not only New Orleans but the entire state of Louisiana as well. In addition you might keep an eye out for the mobile **Info à la Cart** sites around town.

CITY LAYOUT

The French Quarter, where the city began, is a 13-block-long area between Canal Street and Esplanade Avenue running from the Mississippi River to North Rampart Street. Because of the bend in the river, much of the city is laid out at angles that render useless such mundane directions as north, south, east, and west. New Orleans solved this directional problem long ago by simply substituting *riverside, lakeside, uptown,* and *downtown.* It works, and you'll catch on quickly if you keep in mind that North Rampart Street is the "lakeside" boundary of the Quarter, Canal Street marks the beginning of "uptown," and the Quarter is "downtown." As for building numbers, they begin at 100 on either side of Canal. In the Quarter they begin at 400 at the river (that's because four blocks of numbered buildings were lost to the river before the levee was built). Another reminder of Canal Street's boundary role between new and old New Orleans is the fact that street names change when they cross it (that is, Bourbon Street "downtown" becomes Carondelet "uptown").

Maps   You can get decent maps almost anywhere in New Orleans. If you'll need them before you leave home, call the New Orleans Metropolitan Convention and Visitors Bureau (see above) and they'll send them to you. Otherwise, stop by there or the Visitor Information Center when you arrive and pick them up. If you rent a car, be sure to ask for maps of the city—the rental agents have good ones. Major bookstores also sell good city maps. If you're planning excursions outside the city, the places listed above also supply state maps.

NEIGHBORHOODS IN BRIEF

The French Quarter   Made up of about 90 square blocks, this section is also known as the Vieux Carré and is bounded on the south by Canal Street, the west by North Rampart Street, the east by the Mississippi River, and the north by Esplanade Avenue. It is the most historic and the best preserved area in the city.

Canal Street/Central Business District   There's no street more central to the life of New Orleans than Canal—the location of everything is described in reference to its relation to Canal Street. It took its name from a very shallow ditch that was dug along this border of the French Quarter in its early days. Although the ditch was given the rather grand name of canal, it was never large enough to be used for transport.

The Central Business District (CBD) is roughly bounded by Canal Street on the north and the elevated Pontchartrain Expressway (Bus. I-90) to the south, between Loyola Avenue and the Mississippi River. There are pleasant plazas, squares, and parks sprinkled among all the commercial high-rise buildings of the CBD, and some of the most elegant of the luxury hotels are located in this area.

The Warehouse District   With the revitalization of an area once devoted almost entirely to abandoned warehouses into an upscale residential neighborhood, the area between Julia and St. Joseph streets has become a mecca for artists. The area is just loaded with galleries (listed in Chapter 7) that show the works of contemporary artists. The Contemporary Arts Center, 900 Camp St. (see Chapter 6 for a full listing) just beyond St. Joseph toward Howard Avenue, has facilities for presenting not only art exhibitions but also performances. Also in this area, you will find the Louisiana Children's Museum (see "Especially for Kids" in Chapter 6 for more details).

The Garden District   Located uptown and bounded by St. Charles Avenue (lakeside) and Magazine Street (riverside) between Jackson and Louisiana avenues, it remains one of the most beautiful areas in the city because of the old Victorian homes that line the streets. Unfortunately, most of the gardens that used to exist around the outsides of the homes no longer exist and some of the houses are in disrepair, but you can still get some idea of what it used to be like.

The Irish Channel   The area between the Garden District (Magazine Street) and the river is known locally as the Irish Channel because it was home to hundreds of Irish immigrants during the 1800s. These days it is an interesting, although somewhat seedy, section of town. It houses many of New Orleans's poor, just as it did in the early days when Irish immigrants struggled to establish themselves in New Orleans and lived along these streets. An illuminating sidelight to the city's history is the fact that between 1820 and 1860 the more than 100,000 Irish newcomers were considered more "expendable" than costly slaves—many were killed while employed doing dangerous construction work and any other manual labor. In spite of that, there was a toughness and lively spirit that gave the Irish Channel a distinctive neighborhood flavor. Today it is mostly populated by African Americans and Hispanic Americans, and there is still a sort of "street camaraderie" alive here.

Basin Street   You remember Basin Street, of course—the birthplace of jazz. But some people will tell you that Storyville (the red-light district along Basin Street) served only as a place for jazz, which had been around a long time, to come in off the streets. It did that, all right—jazz bands became the house entertainment in the many ornate "sporting palaces" that offered a wide variety of "services," primarily of the sex-for-hire variety. King Oliver, Jelly Roll Morton, and Louis Armstrong were among the jazz greats who got

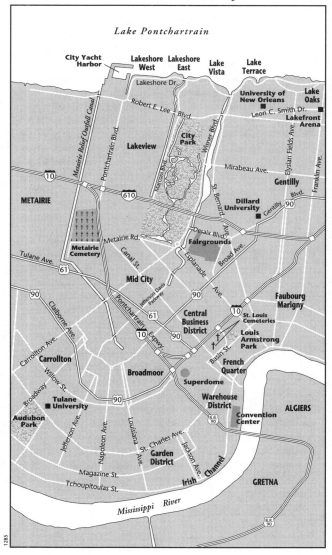

Lake Pontchartrain

City Yacht Harbor
Lakeshore West
Lakeshore East
Lake Vista
Lake Terrace
Lakeshore Dr.
Robert E. Lee Blvd.
University of New Orleans
Lake Oaks
Leon C. Smith Dr.
Lakefront Arena
Metairie Relief Outfall Canal
Pontchartrain Blvd.
Lakeview
City Park
Marconi Blvd.
Wisner Blvd.
Mirabeau Ave.
Elysian Fields Ave.
Franklin Ave.
Gentilly
METAIRIE
St. Bernard Ave.
Dillard University
Gentilly Blvd.
Metairie Cemetery
Metairie Rd.
Desaix Blvd.
Fairgrounds
Broad Ave.
Tulane Ave.
Canal St.
Esplanade Ave.
Mid City
Jefferson Davis Parkway
Faubourg Marigny
Pontchartrain Expwy.
Central Business District
St. Louis Cemeteries
Claiborne Ave.
Carrollton Ave.
Carrollton
Basin St.
Louis Armstrong Park
Willow St.
Broadmoor
French Quarter
Broadway
Superdome
Tulane University
Warehouse District
ALGIERS
Audubon Park
Jefferson Ave.
Louisiana Ave.
Convention Center
Napoleon Ave.
St. Charles Ave.
Jackson Ave.
Garden District
Magazine St.
Tchoupitoulas St.
Irish Channel
GRETNA
Mississippi River

25

Speak Like a Native

The language is English, of course, but in New Orleans it comes with tones, accents, and pronunciations that may surprise you. Don't expect to hear a lot of "y'alls" or other Deep South expressions; be prepared instead for a sort of southern Brooklynese. There are, of course, all sorts of dialects around town, as you'd expect from the variety of ethnic backgrounds represented in New Orleans, but somehow they *all* seem to have developed a little bit along the lines of speech in New York's Brooklyn. Unless you stick to the Garden District and university campuses, you should know before you arrive that "toin" translates to turn, "erl" means oil, and even the most cultured downtowner is likely to slip in "de" for the.

To help you sound less like a "foreigner" as you move around town, here are some words and street names that are given the native twist:

bayou	*BY-you* (a marshy, sluggish stream, usually feeding into a river or lake; also, the swamplands of southern Louisiana)
banquette	*ban-KET* (a French word for bench that means "sidewalk" in New Orleans, since early wooden sidewalks were elevated above muddy streets)
neutral ground	(a uniquely New Orleans term meaning a "median" in the roadway)
Vieux Carré	*view ka-RAY*
Conti Street	*CON-teye*
Burgundy Street	*bur-GUN-dee*
Carondelet Street	*car-ONDE-let* (not *lay*)
Calliope Street	*CAL-i-ope* (not *cal-I-opee*)
Chartres Street	*charters*
Dauphine Street	*daw-FEEN*
Iberville Street	*EYE-bur-vill*
Bienville Street	*bee-EN-vill*
Orleans Street	*or-LEENS*
but	
New Orleans	*noo OR-lyuns* (or, better yet, *nor-luns*)
Tchoupitoulas Street	*chop-a-TOOL-us*
Terpsichore Street	*TURP-sick-ory*

You're sure to hear others that sound peculiar, but don't question, just follow the lead of those who live here.

their start on Basin Street in the brothels between Canal Street and Beauregard Square. Storyville operated with reckless abandon from 1897, when Alderman Sidney Story proposed a plan for the concentration of illegal activities in this area, until an official of the U.S. Navy had it closed down in 1917.

What you'll find today is a far cry from what was there in those rowdy days. A low-income public housing project now sprawls over the site, and statues depicting Latin American heroes dot the landscape. Simón Bolívar presides over the Canal and Basin streets intersection; there's also a statue of Mexico's Benito Juárez with the inscription "Peace is based on the respect of the rights of others"; and finally a likeness of Gen. Francisco Morazón, a hero of Central America, given to the city by Honduras and El Salvador, is last in line at Basin and St. Louis streets.

Faubourg Marigny   *Faubourg* means "suburb," and Marigny is the name of a prominent early New Orleans family. For some years the area (beginning with Frenchmen Street) had been going downhill; these days, however, small businesses, a good hotel (The Frenchmen, see Chapter 4), several good eateries, and many popular music spots are revitalizing Frenchmen Street and its smaller tributaries. Because of Faubourg Marigny's proximity to the Quarter, the restaurants and entertainment there are included with those of the Quarter.

NETWORKS & RESOURCES

For African Americans   The **Greater New Orleans Black Tourism Network** (☎ 504/523-5652) can provide information on tourism that is of interest to black Americans or to others who are interested in African-American culture as it pertains to New Orleans.

For Gay Men & Lesbians   The **Gay and Lesbian Community Center** is located at 816 N. Rampart St. (☎ 504/524-8334). The **NO/AIDS** task force has a 24-hour hotline (☎ 504/945-4000).

Ambush magazine is the Gulf South weekly entertainment/news publication for the gay and lesbian community. You can access *Ambush* through the internet at http://www.ambushmag.com. *Impact Gulf South Gay News* is another popular area publication.

Grace Fellowship (☎ 504/944-9836 or 504/949-2325) and **Vieux Carré Metropolitan Community Church,** 1128 St. Roch (☎ 504/945-5390) are both religious organizations that support gays and lesbians.

For Seniors & Travelers with Disabilities   "Rollin' by the River," a guide to wheelchair-accessible restaurants and clubs in the

French Quarter, is available for a handling fee of $2.25 (they'll send it on receipt of your check or money order) from the **Advocacy Center for the Elderly and Disabled,** 210 O'Keefe Ave., Suite 700, New Orleans, LA 70112 (☎ **504/522-2337**). Seniors are welcome to use this number as well.

For information about specialized transportation systems, call **LIFT** at **504/827-7433.**

2 Getting Around

BY PUBLIC TRANSPORTATION

Discount Passes   You can obtain a **VisiTour** pass that will entitle you to an unlimited number of rides on all streetcar and bus lines. It costs $4 for one day, $8 for three days. Ask at your hotel or guest house where you can get the VisiTour pass. You can also call the **Regional Transit Authority** for information at **504/248-3900.**

By Bus   New Orleans has an excellent public bus system, and you can get complete information on which buses run where by calling **504/248-3900** or by picking up an excellent city map at the Visitor Information Center, 529 St. Ann St. in the French Quarter. All fares at the moment are $1 (you must have exact change, and transfers are an extra 10¢), except for expresses, which are $1.25.

Along the riverfront, buses made up to look like vintage streetcars, affectionately known as the "Ladies in Red," run for 1.9 miles from the Old Mint, across Canal Street, to Riverview. The fare is $1.25, there are convenient stops along the way, and there's ramp access for the disabled—a great step-saver as you explore this lively area of the city.

By Streetcar   One treat you really should allow yourself is the 1¹/₂-hour ride down St. Charles Avenue on the famous old streetcar line, which has been named a national historic landmark. The trolleys run 24 hours a day at frequent intervals, and the fare is $1 each way (you must have exact change). Board at Canal and Carondelet streets (directly across Canal from Bourbon Street in the French Quarter), sit back, and look for landmarks in this part of town.

The end of the line is at Palmer Park and Playground at Clairborne Avenue, but if you want to mount a shopping expedition at the interesting Riverbend Shopping Area (see Chapter 7), get off at Carrollton. It will cost you another $1 for the ride back to Canal Street. If you would like to transfer from the streetcar to a bus it will cost you 10¢.

BY CAR

The following is a list of car-rental agencies with their local and t... free numbers and addresses:

Avis, 2024 Canal St. (☎ **800/331-1212** or 504/523-4317); **Budget Rent-A-Car,** 1317 Canal St. (☎ **800/527-0700** or 504/467-2277); **Dollar Rent-A-Car,** 1910 Airline Hwy., Kenner (☎ **504/467-2285**); **Hertz,** 901 Convention Center Blvd. No. 101 (☎ **800/654-3131** or 504/568-1645); **Swifty Car Rental,** 2300 Canal St. (☎ **504/524-7368**); **Value Rent-A-Car,** 1701 Airline Hwy., Kenner (☎ **504/469-2688**).

Rental rates vary according to the time of your visit and from company to company, so just call ahead and see what rate they can offer you. Try all the agencies; keep asking questions and trying different combinations of dates and promotional offers (reservations clerks are not terribly forthcoming about helping you find the cheapest option). *Note:* If you're staying for a week or more be sure to ask about weekly rates—stay away from the daily rates.

Comparatively speaking, driving in New Orleans isn't too difficult and traffic officers are fairly tolerant of moving violations (which isn't to say that you should disregard traffic rules), but they're absolute murder on illegal parking, handing out tickets right and left. For that reason, I strongly suggest that you put the car away for any French Quarter sightseeing (it's more fun, anyway, on foot) and use it only for longer jaunts out of congested areas. Most hotels provide parking for their guests (although a daily fee is usually charged); smaller hotels or guest houses (particularly in the French Quarter) may not have parking facilities but will be able to direct you to a nearby public garage.

French Quarter driving is more difficult than driving in some other areas of the city. All streets there are one-way, and on weekdays during daylight hours, Royal and Bourbon streets are closed to automobiles between the 300 and 700 blocks. Driving is also trying in the Central Business District, where congested traffic and limited parking make life difficult for the motorist. It is much smarter to park the car and use the public transportation provided in both areas.

BY TAXI

Taxis are plentiful in New Orleans and respond quickly to telephone calls. They can be hailed easily on the street in the French Quarter and some parts of the Central Business District and are usually in place at taxi stands at the larger hotels. Otherwise, telephone and ear in three to five minutes. In my experience, three drivers will get out to open doors for you ride. Rates are $1.70 when you enter the taxi and after. During special events (like Mardi Gras and is $3 per person (or the meter rate if it's greater) you go in the city. The city's most reliable company is **United Cabs** (☎ 504/524-9606).

Touring tip: Most taxis can be hired for an hourly rate for up to five passengers—a hassle-free and economical way for a small group to tour far-flung areas of the city (the lakefront, for example). Out-of-town trips cost double the amount on the meter.

ON FOOT

In my opinion, the *only* way to see the French Quarter (and some parts of the Garden District) is by foot. It's easy to find your way around both of these small areas, and they are crammed with things you won't want to miss. Only by strolling can you really soak up the charm of both these sections. In the Quarter, look through iron gates or down alleyways for glimpses of lovely patios and courtyards and above street level for interesting facades and incredibly delicate, lacy iron railings. Along Bourbon Street, intersperse strolls with stops to listen to live jazz groups playing at open-door saloons—there's nonstop music most of the day. In the Garden District, be sure to allow enough time to drink in the beauty of the formal gardens surrounding the fine old mansions.

BY FERRY

One of New Orleans's nicest treats is absolutely free. It's the 25-minute (round-trip) ferry ride across the Mississippi from the foot of Canal Street to Algiers. It's a joy, whether you go by day for a view of the busy harbor or at night when the lights of the city reflect in the mighty river. If you'd like to do some West Bank driving, the ferry carries both car and foot passengers.

FAST FACTS: New Orleans

Airport   See "Getting There" in Chapter 1.

American Express   The American Express office (☎ 504/586-8201) is located at 158 Baronne St. in the Central Business District.

Baby-Sitters   If your hotel doesn't offer any help in finding child care, try calling **Accent on Children's Arrangements** (☎ 504/524-1227).

Business Hours As far as businesses and stores go, New Orleans is generally a 9 to 5 town. Some stores, particularly in the French Quarter, open late and, as a consequence, stay open later. Just call before you go to be sure. Banking hours are generally 9am to 3pm weekdays, although some banks stay open later one day per week and some offer limited Saturday hours. There is no official closure law for bars, so many stay open into the wee hours.

Car Rentals See "Getting Around," earlier in this chapter.

Climate See "When to Go" in Chapter 1.

Convention Center The **Ernest N. Morial Convention Center** is located at 900 Convention Center Blvd. (☎ 504/582-3000).

Emergencies For fire, ambulance, and police, just dial 911 in an emergency.

Hospitals Should you become ill during your New Orleans visit, most major hotels have in-house staff doctors on call 24 hours a day. If there's not one available in your hotel or guest house, call or go to the Emergency Room at **Ochsner Medical Institutions,** 880 Commerce Rd. W. (☎ 504/842-3460), or the **Tulane University Medical Center,** 1415 Tulane Ave. (☎ 504/588-5800).

Information See "Visitor Information," earlier in this chapter.

Liquor Laws Alcoholic beverages are available in New Orleans around the clock, seven days a week. You are allowed to drink on the street, but only as long as your libation is in a plastic cup or container. Although the legal drinking age is 21 years, I've seen people much younger taking their seats at the bar.

One warning: Although the police may look the other way if they see a pedestrian who's had a few too many (as long as he or she is peaceful and not bothering anyone else), they have no tolerance at all for those who are intoxicated behind the wheel.

Newspapers/Magazines To find out what's going on around town, pick up a copy of the *Times-Picayune* or *New Orleans Magazine. Offbeat Publications* is a monthly guide to the city's evening entertainment, art galleries, and special events. It can be found in most hotels. *Where Magazine* and *Arrive Magazine,* also published monthly, are good resources for visitors. *This Week Magazine* is an informative weekly publication for visitors.

Photographic Needs   One of the city's most complete camera shops is the **K&B Camera Center,** 227 Dauphine St. (☎ **504/ 524-2266**), with a wide selection of cameras and other electronics, as well as film and camera and darkroom supplies. Fast film developing is also available. It is open Monday through Friday from 8am to 6pm, Saturday from 8am to 2pm. **Fox Photo Labs,** 414 Canal St. (☎ **504/529-6120**), and **French Quarter Camera,** 809 Decatur St. (☎ **504/529-2974**), also offer one-hour film processing.

Post Office   The main post office is located at 701 Loyola Ave. There's also a post office in the World Trade Center. If you're in the Vieux Carré, you'll find a post office at 1022 Iberville St. There's another one at 610 S. Maestri Place.

If you've got something large or fragile to send home and you don't feel like hunting around for packing materials, go to **The Wooden Box Packing and Shipping Co.,** 816 South Peters (☎ **504/568-0281**), or **Prytania Mail Services,** 5500 Prytania St. (☎ **504/897-0877**); both places will pack and ship items for a surcharge.

Safety   While visiting any unfamiliar city you should be careful, but in New Orleans in particular, don't walk alone at night, and do not go into the cemeteries alone at any time during the day or night. Ask around locally before you go anywhere—people will tell you if you should take a cab instead of walking or taking public transportation.

Taxes   Sales tax in New Orleans is 9%. An additional 2% tax is added to hotel bills for a total of 11%.

Taxis   See "Getting Around" in this chapter.

Time & Temperature   Call **504/465-9212** for weather and **504/976-1111** for the time.

Time Zone   New Orleans observes central standard time, the same time zone as Chicago.

Transit Information   Local bus routes and schedules can be obtained from the **RTA Ride Line** (☎ **504/248-3900**).

Useful Telephone Numbers   You can reach the **Travelers Aid Society** at **504/525-8726. Union Passenger Terminal,** 1001 Loyola Ave., provides bus information (☎ **504/524-7571**) and train information (☎ **504/528-1610**).

4

Accommodations

*D*espite the annual influx of hundreds of thousands of visitors needing a place to stay, New Orleans has managed to keep historic districts, such as the French Quarter, free of high-rise monstrosities. Indeed, it is almost impossible to tell if some of the new French Quarter hotels have been built from scratch or lovingly placed inside the shell of an older building, so faithful has been the dedication to preserving the Quarter's architectural style. Even motor hotels (which have alleviated the ever-present problem of on-street parking) have a look that is distinctly New Orleans.

You'll find those high-rise hotels, of course, but they're more appropriately located uptown, in commercial sections, where they seem to fit just fine.

Some of the new hotels about which you might inquire in 1997 are the Queen and Crescent Hotel, the Omni Crescent Hotel, and the Wyndham Riverfront Hotel. They're not yet open as this book goes to press, but they promise to be quite lovely.

As for guest houses, they really do make you feel like a guest. Presided over by New Orleanians (or others, charmed by the city, who picked up and moved here) and imbued with a special brand of hospitality, many are furnished with antiques and all provide a very homelike atmosphere. After spending time in numerous New Orleans guest houses, I'd recommend them over hotel-style accommodations.

A sort of passkey to the lively people who live in New Orleans is the **Bed and Breakfast Reservation Service** (☎ **800/729-4640** or 504/488-4640). Personable Hazell Boyce can put you up in luxury in 19th-century, turn-of-the-century, or modern residences. Or you can opt for a cottage in the French Quarter or Garden District areas. Prices range from $35 to $225 single or double occupancy, and she delights in arranging modest lodging for students. Hazell will send you free listings that include rates and locations upon request.

Advance reservations (a good idea whatever the season) are a must during spring, fall, and winter months, when the city is crowded. If your trip will coincide with Mardi Gras or Jazz Fest, it isn't an exaggeration to say that you should book as far as a year in advance. Sugar Bowl week and other festival times also flood New Orleans with visitors and require advance planning for accommodations, and of course, there's always a chance that a big convention will be in town, making it difficult to find a room. It's conceivable that you might run across a cancellation and get a last-minute booking, but the chances are remote, to say the least. You should also be aware that rates frequently jump more than a notch or two for Mardi Gras and other festival times, and in some cases there's a four- or five-night minimum requirement.

If you want to miss the crowd and lodging squeeze that mark the big festivals, consider coming in the month immediately following Carnival (after Fat Tuesday, the last day before Lent) or in the summer months (though they are often unbearably hot and muggy) when the streets are not nearly as thronged.

Since I am convinced that the only place to stay is in the French Quarter—the very heart and soul of New Orleans—I'm listing accommodations there first. But if circumstances make another location more desirable for you, you'll find listings outside the Quarter in this chapter as well. Note that there are no recommendable inexpensive hotels in the French Quarter. If you're on a budget and must stay here, consider a guest house. On the whole, however, you will have a better selection of inexpensive lodgings outside the Quarter. Note that there are two hostels in New Orleans; both are listed at the end of this chapter.

Rates given are for double rooms and do not include the city's 11% hotel tax. Reduced single-occupancy rates are often offered; inquire when you make reservations. Unless otherwise noted in a particular hotel or guest house listing, all accommodations in New Orleans have private baths.

1 Best Bets

- **Best for a Romantic Getaway:** The **Melrose Mansion,** 937 Esplanade Ave. (☎ **504/944-2255**), is an excellent choice. Your visit will begin with a ride in a chauffeured stretch limousine, and when you arrive at the Melrose you'll be greeted by the butler. Rooms are furnished with exquisite antiques and some feature deep Jacuzzi tubs. Service is impeccable.
- **Best Moderately Priced Hotel:** For my money, the **Bourbon Orleans Hotel,** 717 Orleans St. (☎ **504/523-2222**), is the best

moderately priced hotel in New Orleans. It's centrally located, has excellent amenities, and rivals some of the city's more expensive hotels in elegance and quality of service.

- **Best Guest House Value:** At the **McKendrick-Breaux House,** 1474 Magazine St. (☎ **504/586-1700**), you get the kind of service you'd expect at a larger, more expensive hotel, and your hosts seem to know instinctively just how much (or how little) attention you need. Rooms are exceptionally large; the claw-foot bathtubs in the rooms in the main house are an added luxury.

- **Best Location:** If you want to stay right in the French Quarter, you'll be hard pressed to find a hotel better located than the **Omni Royal Orleans,** 621 St. Louis St. (☎ **800/THE-OMNI** or 504/529-5333). It happens to be one of the city's most elegant hostelries, and it also features the Rib Room, one of New Orleans's best restaurants.

- **Best Modern Hotel:** You'll want for nothing in the luxury, high-rise **Hotel Inter-Continental,** 444 St. Charles Ave. (☎ **800/ 327-0200** or 504/525-5566). All rooms, even the standard ones, have such special touches as minibars and mini-TVs in the dressing alcoves. There's a health club with pool, butler service on the executive floor, business services, and an excellent restaurant here as well.

- **Best Health Club:** Hands down, this distinction belongs to the the **New Orleans Hilton Riverside Hotel,** 2 Poydras St. (☎ **800/445-8667** or 504/561-0500). Their Rivercenter Racquet and Health Club features outdoor and indoor tennis courts, squash and racquetball courts, a rooftop jogging track, aerobics classes, tanning beds, massage, a hair salon, and a golf studio.

- **Best Gay-Friendly Hotel:** The **New Orleans Guest House,** 1118 Ursulines St. (☎ **504/566-1177**), located on the outer edge of the French Quarter, just off North Rampart Street, is a favorite with the visiting gay and lesbian community (though the clientele is not entirely gay). A lush courtyard with bubbling fountains and unique garden statues, individually decorated rooms, and reasonable rates also makes this one of the best buys in the city.

- **In a Category by Itself:** Of all the hotels in New Orleans, **The Windsor Court,** 300 Gravier St. (☎ **800/262-2662** or 504/ 523-6000), stands head and shoulders above the rest. The hotel's lovely public areas are a treasure trove of fine art. Most guest rooms are suites featuring Italian marble bathrooms, fine fabrics, balconies or bay windows, living rooms, kitchenettes, and dressing rooms. If you choose a two-bedroom penthouse suite, you'll have the added luxury of your own private library and a terrace that overlooks the mighty Mississippi.

2 In the French Quarter

VERY EXPENSIVE

✪ **Omni Royal Orleans.** 621 St. Louis St., New Orleans, LA 70140. ☎ **800/ THE-OMNI** in the U.S. and Canada or 504/529-5333. Fax 504/529-7089. 346 rms, 16 suites. A/C TV TEL. $175–$250 double; $350–$1,000 suite. Children 17 and under free with parents. AE, CB, DC, DISC, MC, V. Valet parking $14 per day with in/out privileges.

Considered *the* place to stay by many veteran visitors, the elegant Omni Royal Orleans is certainly one of the most beautiful French Quarter hotels. The present-day hotel opened its doors in 1960 on the site of the 1836 St. Louis Exchange Hotel, one of this country's most splendid hostelries of the mid-19th century. The St. Louis Exchange was a center of New Orleans social life until the final years of the Civil War, when it first became a hospital for wounded soldiers from both the North and the South, then served for a time as the state capitol building and a meeting place of the carpetbagger legislature, and finally was destroyed by a 1915 hurricane. In its heyday of gala soirees and eminent visitors, it was also the innovator of the "free lunch" for noontime drinkers, establishing a tradition of top-notch noontime cuisine that survives even today.

The Omni Royal Orleans has proved a worthy successor, with a lobby of marble and brass and crystal chandeliers. Furnishings are truly sumptuous in the guest rooms. All rooms come equipped with umbrellas, irons, and ironing boards, and bathrooms include such amenities as terry-cloth bathrobes and makeup mirrors.

Dining/Entertainment: The classic Rib Room is a favorite dining spot for many locals (see Chapter 5), and there's soft music after 8pm in the elegant Esplanade Lounge. Touché Bar offers light meals and excellent mint juleps. The rooftop, poolside, palm tree–bordered La Riviera bar and restaurant is a terrific lunch spot, with unobstructed views of the French Quarter.

Services: Concierge, baby-sitting, emergency mending and pressing services, complimentary shoe shine, nightly turn-down service, 24-hour room service.

French Quarter Accommodations

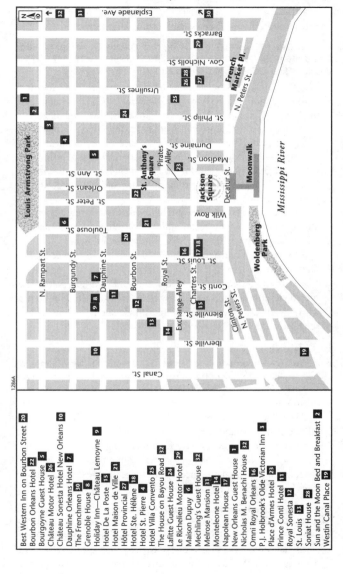

37

Facilities: Health club, heated pool, beauty and barber shops, florist, sundries shop and newsstand, business center.

Westin Canal Place. 100 Iberville St., New Orleans, LA 70130. ☎ **800/228-3000** or 504/566-7006. 438 rms. A/C MINIBAR TV TEL. $235–$298 double. AE, CB, DC, DISC, MC, V. Parking $12.

The Westin Canal Place has one of the most convenient locations in town—right on the Mississippi River on the Canal Street edge of the French Quarter. Sweeping views are a big plus here. The 11th-floor lobby is a masterpiece of Carrara marble, fine paintings, and antiques. Each room has a marble foyer and bath, fine furnishings, as well as phones with call waiting and voice mail. The Westin Guest Office program (for an additional $20) includes use of an in-room combination copier/printer/fax machine, free office supplies, and the use of an in-room coffeemaker.

Dining/Entertainment: The lobby makes a lovely setting for afternoon tea. The Green Bar and The Riverbend Grill restaurant are just steps away. There is also a Sunday jazz brunch.

Services: Full concierge service, 24-hour room service, multilingual staff.

Facilities: Heated pool, privileges at a nearby 18-hole golf course, special elevator descending directly to Canal Place shopping center where guests can enjoy use of the Health Center or visit the barbershop, beauty salon, and stores.

EXPENSIVE

Best Western Inn on Bourbon Street. 541 Bourbon St., New Orleans, LA 70130. ☎ **800/535-7891** or 504/524-7611. 186 rms. A/C TV TEL. $155–$235 double. AE, DC, DISC, MC, V. Parking $9.

All rooms have a Deep South decor and king-size or double beds, and some have balconies overlooking Bourbon Street. Both the Sing-a-Long piano bar and the Bourbon Street Cafeteria (a self-service restaurant featuring Creole and Cajun cooking) are notable. There is a fitness center, and the hotel offers room service, concierge services, and laundry/valet service. Prices hinge on whether your room faces Bourbon Street or has a balcony.

Chateau Sonesta Hotel New Orleans. 800 Iberville St., New Orleans, LA. ☎ **800/SONESTA** or 504/586-0800. 255 rms. A/C MINIBAR TV TEL. $145–$215 double, $275–$575 suite. Extra person $35. AE, MC, V. Valet parking $14.

The Chateau Sonesta Hotel, one of the city's newest hostelries, still maintains its 1913 facade and is convenient to the French Quarter. Guest rooms are large and many feature balconies overlooking either

Bourbon or Dauphine streets. Videos are available for rental. Phone systems, with voice mail, conference calling, data port, and modem capabilities are state of the art.

Dining/Entertainment: La Chatelaine Restaurant and The Clock Bar are open daily.

Services: Concierge, room service, baby-sitting service, nightly turndown.

Facilities: Indoor and outdoor pools, exercise room, gift shop.

Dauphine Orleans Hotel. 415 Dauphine St., New Orleans, LA 70112. ☎ **800/521-7111** or 504/586-1800. Fax 504/586-1409. 109 rms. A/C MINIBAR TV TEL. $145–$190 double; $170–$370 suite; $150–$220 patio suite. Rates include continental breakfast. Extra person $15. Children under 12 free in parents' room. AE, MC, V. Valet parking $12.

There's a casual elegance at the Dauphine Orleans Hotel. All rooms have recently been upgraded with marble bathrooms (equipped with bathrobes and hair dryers), new solid wood headboards and feather pillows on the beds, and upgraded furnishings, making the Dauphine Orleans one of the French Quarter's loveliest properties. There are three secluded courtyards at the Dauphine, and history lurks around every corner. The hotel's main building was once the studio of the famous John James Audubon, and the "Patio Suites" across the street from the main building were originally built in 1834 as the home of New Orleans merchant Samuel Herrmann.

In 1991, when the cottages, located adjacent to the main hotel, were renovated, many intriguing aspects of the building were uncovered. The nails that can now be seen in the wood posts are thought to have come from the famous Lafitte's Blacksmith Shoppe. Hidden fireplaces have been uncovered, and in a room that was once the kitchen, antique pots and pans were discovered under the floor. While all of the rooms here are nice, I am partial to the cottage rooms.

Dining/Entertainment: May Baily's, the hotel's bar, was once a notorious "sporting house" (brothel), and guests are given a copy of the original 1857 license, which still hangs on the wall. The Coffee Lounge is where continental breakfast is served daily from 6:30 to 11am. Complimentary afternoon tea is also served daily from 3 to 5pm.

Services: Complimentary French Quarter and downtown transportation, morning paper delivered to your door.

Facilities: Pool, guest library, small fitness room.

Hotel Maison de Ville. 727 Toulouse St., New Orleans, LA 70130. ☎ **504/ 561-5858.** 23 rms. A/C MINIBAR TV TEL. $165–$205 double; $375–$525 cottage. AE, MC, V. Valet parking $17.

Unique among New Orleans's luxury hotels is the small, European-style Hotel Maison de Ville. Dating from before 1742, the Maison has been restored to an old-time elegance marked by marble fireplaces, fine French antiques, and gilt-framed mirrors. Guest rooms surround a brick courtyard (one of the loveliest in the Quarter) with a tiered fountain and palm trees. It was here, at one of the wrought-iron tables, that Tennessee Williams reworked *A Streetcar Named Desire;* his usual room was today's room 9. Another famous tenant, John Audubon, lived in one of the seven cottages now operated by the hotel while painting the Louisiana portion of his *Birds of America.* The cottages, with brick walls, beamed ceilings, and slate or brick floors, are furnished with antiques and reflect a warm country elegance. All rooms are equipped with VCRs.

Dining/Entertainment: The Maison's service includes a breakfast of fresh orange juice, croissants or muffins, and steaming chicory coffee served on a silver tray in your room, in the parlor, or on the patio. Complimentary sherry and port are served in the afternoon and evening. The Bistro, the hotel's restaurant, is intimate and inviting.

Services: Morning and evening newspapers delivered to your room; shoe-polishing service.

Maison Dupuy. 1001 Toulouse St., New Orleans, LA 70112. ☎ **800/ 535-9177** or 504/586-8000. Fax 504/525-5334. 198 rms, 10 suites. A/C TV TEL. $95–$205 deluxe double; $250–$800 suite. AE, DC, MC, V. Valet parking $12 when available.

Maison Dupuy is a lovely hotel comprising seven town houses. It's ideally located for French Quarter sightseeing and is the perfect size for those who like their privacy but also like to be recognized by the staff. Rooms are quite large, and each has a desk, comfortable armchairs, and either two double beds or one king-size bed. All have modern bathrooms with standard amenities, and some have balconies that face either the courtyard or the street. In the courtyard you can relax, swim, enjoy a cocktail, or just take in the beautiful surroundings.

Dining/Entertainment: The hotel's restaurant, Le Bon Creole, serves breakfast, lunch, and dinner. The hotel also does a Sunday "Champagne Jazz Brunch Buffet." The Cabaret Lautrec Lounge has live entertainment and is a perfect place to relax. There is also a courtyard patio bar that is open during fair weather.

Services: Room service, twice-daily maid service, same-day laundry and dry cleaning.

Facilities: Heated outdoor pool, health club.

Monteleone Hotel. 214 Royal St., New Orleans, LA 70140. ☎ **800/535-9595** or 504/523-3341. 600 rms. A/C TV TEL. $145–$210 doubledouble or king double; $290–$400 suite. Extra person $25. Children under 18 free in parents' room. Package rates available. AE, CB, DC, MC, V. Parking $11.

The largest French Quarter hotel, the Monteleone has been operated by four generations of Monteleones. Covering almost an entire block, it seems to keep expanding over the years without losing its trademark charm. Service at the Monteleone is surprisingly personal for a hotel this large. Accommodations range from luxurious, antique-filled suites to more modern, comfortable family rooms.

Dining/Entertainment: Le Café restaurant is a favorite with native New Orleanians, and the revolving Carousel Bar also draws the locals.

Services: Room service.

Facilities: Heated rooftop swimming pool (open year-round) and fitness center.

Royal Sonesta. 300 Bourbon St., New Orleans, LA 70140. ☎ **800/766-3782** or 504/586-0300. 500 rms. A/C MINIBAR TV TEL. $160–$280 double; $325–$1,100 suite. Package and seasonal rates may be available. AE, CB, DC, DISC, MC, V. Parking $14.

The Royal Sonesta is adorned with lacy New Orleans balconies, and its rooms are furnished with period reproduction pieces. Many overlook inner patios or the pool, and these are preferable to rooms facing Bourbon Street, which can be noisy. This is an ideal French Quarter location—within walking distance of almost everything.

Dining/Entertainment: Begue's restaurant carries on the tradition of an older New Orleans eating spot of the same name, while Desire offers fresh seafood and an oyster bar. The Can Can Cafe features live Dixieland jazz.

Services: Concierge, room service (until 2am).

Facilities: Pool, exercise room, business center.

St. Louis. 730 Bienville St., New Orleans, LA 70130. ☎ **800/535-9706** or 504/581-7300. 70 rms. A/C TV TEL. $164–$294 double; $324–$755 suite. Children under 12 free in parents' room. AE, CB, DC, MC, V. Valet parking $12.

Another lovely small hotel right in the heart of the French Quarter is the St. Louis. The building surrounds a lush, fountained courtyard and is decorated in high Parisian style, with antique furniture, crystal chandeliers, and gilt-framed original oil paintings. Some rooms have private balconies overlooking Bienville Street, and all overlook the central courtyard. Suites have private courtyards.

Dining/Entertainment: This is the home of an elegant, four-star French restaurant, Louis XVI (see Chapter 5 for a detailed description).

Services: Concierge, room service, complimentary daily newspaper.

✪ **Soniat House.** 1133 Chartres St., New Orleans, LA 70116. ☎ **800/544-8808** or 504/522-0570. Fax 504/522-7208. 31 rms. A/C TV TEL. $145–$235 standard room; $235–$375 suite; $550 two-bedroom suite. AE, MC, V. Valet parking $14 per day.

Built in 1829 by wealthy plantation owner Joseph Soniat Dufossat, the Soniat House is an interesting combination of Creole style and Greek Revival detail. Rodney and Frances Smith purchased the three-story house in 1982 and have done an excellent job of creating the perfect blend of guest house and hotel.

The doorman will welcome you through the impressive plant-lined carriageway that leads to a fountained courtyard (breakfast is served here after 9am upon request). Most of the rooms have balconies and face the courtyard. All rooms are different in size and decor; furnished with French, English, and Louisiana antiques; and feature polished hardwood floors covered with antique Oriental rugs. Also, all have phones in the bathrooms, and some hold paintings on loan from the New Orleans Museum of Art. In 1995 seven new suites were added to the Soniat House in the renovated Soniat family town house (located directly across Chartres Street from main buildings). All have Jacuzzi baths, custom decor, and antique furnishings. Children over 12 are welcome in rooms that accommodate three persons.

Dining/Entertainment: Available every morning after 7am is a "southern continental" breakfast. It consists of freshly baked homemade biscuits, strawberry preserves (specially made for the Soniat House), fresh orange juice, and café au lait; it's $7 extra but worth every penny. There is a fully stocked honor bar in the parlor next to the reception area.

Services: Same-day cleaning and laundry service; evening turndown; 24-hour concierge.

MODERATE

Ⓢ **Bourbon Orleans Hotel.** 717 Orleans St., New Orleans, LA 70116. ☎ **504/523-2222.** Fax 504/525-8166. 161 rms, 50 suites. A/C MINIBAR TV

TEL. $115–$150 petit queen or twin; $135–$225 deluxe king or double/double; $150–$225 junior suite; $210–$325 town house suite; $230–$400 town house with balcony. Extra person $20. AE, DC, DISC, MC, V. Parking $12.

You can't miss the Bourbon Orleans Hotel; it takes up an entire block of the French Quarter. The Orleans Ballroom, located within, dates from the 1800s and is the oldest part of the hotel. It was constructed in 1815 as a venue for the city's masquerade, carnival, and quadroon balls. In 1881 the building was sold to the Sisters of the Holy Family, who were members of the South's first order of African-American nuns. The sisters converted the ballroom into a school, and there they remained for 80 years until the building was sold to real estate developers from Baton Rouge who turned it into an apartment hotel.

Today, the hotel occupies three buildings and has recently undergone a $6 million renovation. Public spaces are lavishly decorated with gorgeous chandeliers, Oriental rugs, and marble flooring, and guest rooms have recently been completely redecorated, and a state-of-the-art movie system is available in each. Coffeemakers are supplied in all the rooms, and you can order room service through your TV. A voice-mail system is operational in all guest rooms. There are standard-size rooms, as well as bilevel suites that have a living room with a pull-out queen sofa. Bathrooms are outfitted with Italian marble, telephones, and hair dryers.

Café Lafayette is the hotel's restaurant, and there is an elegant lobby bar that features a nightly cocktail hour. Additional amenities include room service, same-day dry cleaning, business service, nightly shoe shine, daily morning newspaper, and a pool.

⑤ Château Motor Hotel. 1001 Chartres St., New Orleans, LA 70116. ☎ **504/524-9636.** 45 rms. A/C TV TEL. $84–$104 double. Rates include continental breakfast. Seniors receive 10% discount. AE, CB, DC, MC, V. Free parking.

The Château Motor Hotel is one of the best buys in town. Each room is distinctively decorated. Some have king-size four-poster beds, while others feature painted iron beds, and all have armchairs and/or couches. There are even a few bed/living-room combinations. Its outdoor swimming pool is surrounded by a flagstone-paved courtyard dotted with chaise lounges. Continental breakfast and the morning newspaper are complimentary daily.

The Frenchmen. 417 Frenchmen St., New Orleans, LA 70116. ☎ **800/831-1781** or 504/948-2166. 27 rms. A/C TV TEL. $84–$135 double. Rates include breakfast. AE, MC, V. Free parking.

Situated in two 19th-century buildings, which were once grand New Orleans homes, the Frenchmen is a small inn with an excellent reputation. As you walk in, its elegant lobby sets the tone, and each of the rooms is individually decorated and furnished with beautiful antiques. Standard rooms have one double bed, some rooms have private balconies, and others have a loft bedroom with a sitting area. A pool and Jacuzzi are located in the inn's tropical courtyard. Restaurants, shops, and nightlife are just steps away from this secluded hotel.

Holiday Inn—Château LeMoyne. 301 Dauphine St., New Orleans, LA 70112. ☎ **800/HOLIDAY** or 504/581-1303. 171 rms. A/C TV TEL. $150–$185. Extra person $25. AE, CB, DC, DISC, MC, V. Valet parking $10.

Although this is a Holiday Inn, it is so distinctly French Quarter that you'd never associate it with the ubiquitous roadside chain. Housed in buildings more than a century old, with arched colonnades and winding staircases, the place exudes character and charm. Patios and converted slave-quarter suites add to the old New Orleans flavor, and bedrooms are furnished in a comfortable traditional style. There's a restaurant on the premises for breakfast only, otherwise it's room service until 10pm. There's also a bar and a swimming pool. If you plan to do much sightseeing or business outside the French Quarter, the Château LeMoyne's location is ideal—only minutes away from the Central Business District and the streetcar that takes you to the Garden District. And, of course, anything in the Quarter is within easy walking distance.

Hotel de la Poste. 316 Chartres St., New Orleans, LA 70130. ☎ **800/448-4927** or 504/581-1200. Fax 504/523-2910. 100 rms. A/C TV TEL. $150–$185 double; $180–$215 junior suite. Children under 16 free in parents' room. Package rates, AAA and senior-citizen discounts available. AE, CB, DC, MC, V. Valet parking $12.

Right in the heart of the Quarter, the recently remodeled Hotel de la Poste has spacious and comfortable rooms, most of which overlook either the courtyard and fountain or one of the more interesting French Quarter streets. The courtyard has a magnificent staircase leading to a second-level outdoor patio. There is an outdoor pool, *USA Today* is delivered daily to your room, all guest room phones feature voice mail and data ports, and complimentary coffee, tea, and apples are available. Services include valet laundry service, concierge tours, room service, a 24-hour bellman, and baby-sitting. Also within the hotel is Ristorante Bacco, run by sibling restaurateurs Cindy and Ralph Brennan. Location, accommodations, and service are all first rate.

Hôtel Provincial. 1024 Chartres St., New Orleans, LA 70116. ☎ **800/535-7922** or 504/581-4995. Fax 504/581-1018. 100 rms. A/C TV TEL. $90–$175 double. Summer package rates are available. AE, CB, DC, MC, V. Parking available on premises.

There are no fewer than five patios—and each is a jewel—at the family owned Hôtel Provincial. The building dates from the 1830s, and rooms are high-ceilinged, each one decorated distinctively with imported French and authentic Creole antiques. My favorite holds a huge carved mahogany double bed with a high overhanging canopy topped by a carved tiara. Gaslights on the patios and the overall feeling of graciousness make this establishment a real delight, a tranquil refuge from the rigors of sightseeing or nighttime revelry. The pleasant restaurant serves breakfast, lunch, and dinner at moderate prices.

Hotel Ste. Hélène. 508 Chartres St., New Orleans, LA 70130. ☎ **800/348-3888** or 504/522-5014. Fax 504/523-7140. 26 rms. A/C TV TEL. $125–$185 double. Rates include continental breakfast. AE, CB, DC, DISC, JCB, MC, V. Parking is about $14 in nearby lot.

Located right in the middle of the French Quarter, not far from Jackson Square, Hotel Ste. Hélène is a no-frills kind of place with an ideal location. Here you can be a part of the action, but far enough away from Bourbon Street to escape the noise and mayhem that begins just before dusk.

With a trickling fountain, greenery, and exposed brick walls, the inner courtyard is the center of the hotel. The outer courtyard has a flagstone patio with cast-iron tables and chairs at which you can have your breakfast every morning. The rooms vary mainly in size and the type of bed they hold; all are clean and comfortable. The superior rooms have king-size beds and balconies. There is also a small swimming pool.

Hotel St. Pierre. 911 Burgundy St., New Orleans, LA 70116. ☎ **800/535-7785,** 800/225-4040, or 504/524-4401. Fax 504/524-6800. 74 rms and suites. A/C TV TEL. $120 double; $135 king or double-double; $139–$169 suite. Rates include morning coffee and doughnuts. Extra person $20. Children under 12 are free in parents' room. AE, CB, DC, DISC, MC, V. Free parking.

The Hotel St. Pierre is only two blocks from Bourbon Street. Guest rooms here are surrounded by beautiful courtyards, and because of the original floor plan of the old Creole home, room sizes vary greatly throughout the hotel. Some of the rooms are located in the old slave quarters, and most of them have king-size beds. Half of the rooms have fireplaces. A breakfast of coffee and doughnuts is available each morning in the breakfast room. There are two outdoor pools.

Hotel Villa Convento. 616 Ursulines St., New Orleans, LA 70116. ☎ **504/ 522-1793.** Fax 504/524-1902. 24 rms. A/C TV TEL. $79–$95 double; $105 and $125 suite. Additional person $10 extra. Rates include continental breakfast. AE, CB, DC, DISC, MC, V. Parking is available in public parking area at the riverfront ($15 per day).

The Hotel Villa Convento in many respects resembles a guest house because of the personal touch of its owners/operators, the Campo family. The building is a Creole town house with individually decorated rooms. Some open to the tropical patio, others open to the street; many have balconies. The lovely "loft" rooms are unique family quarters, each with a king-size bed on the entry level and twin beds in the loft. A continental breakfast is served in the courtyard, and guests who prefer breakfast in bed may have a tray to take it to their rooms.

Le Richelieu Motor Hotel. 1234 Chartres St., New Orleans, LA 70116. ☎ **800/535-9653** in the U.S. and Canada or 504/529-2492. Fax 504/ 524-8179. 88 rms, 17 suites. A/C TV TEL. $95–$140 double; $160–$475 suite. Extra person or child $15. Ask about French Quarter Explorer and Honeymoon packages. AE, CB, DC, DISC, JCB, MC, V. Free parking.

Le Richelieu Motor Hotel is housed in what was once a row mansion and then a macaroni factory. Most rooms have brass ceiling fans, many have refrigerators and balconies, and all overlook either the French Quarter or the courtyard. Bathrooms are large and are outfitted with hair dryers. There's a pool in the large courtyard, with lunch service poolside. The Terrace Café is the hotel's restaurant, and the Terrace Lounge is the bar. Le Richelieu is the only French Quarter motel with free self-parking on the premises—you keep your car keys, so there's no wait for an attendant to bring your car. Local calls are also free.

Place d'Armes Hotel. 625 St. Ann St., New Orleans, LA 70116. ☎ **800/ 366-2743** or 504/524-4531. 79 rms. A/C TV TEL. $100–$160 double. Rates include continental breakfast. AE, CB, DC, DISC, MC, V. 24-hour parking next door for $10.

The lovely Place d'Armes has one of the most magnificent courtyards in the Quarter, as well as a swimming pool. All rooms are homey and furnished in traditional style; many are wallpapered. Be sure that you ask, however, for a room with a window when you reserve—there are some interior rooms without windows. The complimentary breakfast is served in a breakfast room, and the location, just off Jackson Square, makes sightseeing a breeze.

Prince Conti Hotel. 830 Conti St., New Orleans, LA 70112. ☎ **800/ 366-2743** or 504/529-4172. 49 rms. A/C TV TEL. $120–$150 double. Rates include continental breakfast. AE, DC, DISC, MC, V. Valet parking $10.

The Prince Conti has a small lobby beautifully furnished in the French château fashion and sports the delicate iron grillwork lining the outside of the second-story rooms. The nicest things, though, are the friendly, helpful staff and the comfortable guest rooms, many furnished with antiques and period reproductions. A continental breakfast is served in the hotel's breakfast room. The restaurant is open Tuesday through Saturday from 5pm.

GUEST HOUSES
EXPENSIVE

Grenoble House. 329 Dauphine St., New Orleans, LA 70112. ☎ **504/ 522-1331.** 17 suites. A/C TV TEL. $185–$285 one-bedroom suite; $235–$375 two-bedroom suite. Rates include continental breakfast. Weekly rates available. AE, MC, V. Parking is available at nearby lot.

The suites at Grenoble House are beautifully and uniquely furnished with a mix of fine antiques and the best of modern fittings—all have fully equipped kitchens. This is an old French Quarter town house built around a courtyard that features a swimming pool with heated whirlpool spa and a barbecue pit. Suites all have king- or queen-size beds, and there's a sofa bed in each living room. Service is very personal and attentive—they'll book theater tickets, restaurant tables, and sightseeing tours and even arrange for a gourmet dinner to be brought to your suite or for a private cocktail party on the patio if you want to entertain friends.

MODERATE

Lafitte Guest House. 1003 Bourbon St., New Orleans, LA 70116. ☎ **800/ 331-7971** or 504/581-2678. 14 rms. A/C TV TEL. $85–$165 double. Rates include continental breakfast. Extra person $22.20. AE, DC, MC, V. Parking $7.50.

If you think a Bourbon Street address automatically means a noisy, honky-tonk environment, think again. The Lafitte Guest House is located beyond the hullabaloo in a quiet, pleasant residential area of the Quarter. The three-story brick building, with wrought-iron balconies on the second and third floors, was constructed in 1849 and has been completely restored. There are marble fireplaces, exposed brick walls, and 14-foot ceilings. Rooms are furnished with a blend of modern reproduction pieces and beautiful Victorian antiques, and each room is individually sized and decorated. A continental breakfast of fresh juice, croissants, jam, butter, and coffee or tea; wine and cheese in the parlor during the "happy hour"; and the daily newspaper are all included in the room rate.

⑤ New Orleans Guest House. 1118 Ursulines St., New Orleans, LA 70116. ☎ **504/566-1177.** 14 rms. A/C TV. $79–$89 queen or twin; $89–$99 king or two full beds. Rates include continental breakfast. Extra person $25. AE, MC, V. Free parking.

Located just on the fringe of the French Quarter, across North Rampart Street, the hot pink New Orleans Guest House is impossible to miss. Ray Cronk and Alvin Payne have been running this renovated Creole cottage, dating from 1848, for more than 10 years now. There are rooms in the main house and some in what used to be the old slave quarters. Rooms in the slave quarters are a little smaller than the ones in the main house, but I actually prefer the smaller ones because they all open onto the lush courtyard. There is a new covered breakfast room with an outdoor patio where you'll be served croissants, fruit, and coffee, tea, or hot chocolate at cozy white-clothed tables. Also located in the courtyard is a beer machine, soda machine, and an ice maker.

✪ P. J. Holbrook's Olde Victorian Inn. 914 North Rampart St. (near the corner of St. Philip St., next door to the Landmark Hotel), New Orleans, LA 70116. ☎ **800/725-2446** or 504/522-2446. 6 rms. A/C. $115–$170 double. Rates include full breakfast. Senior-citizen discount. Weekly rates available. AE, MC, V. Parking on street only.

P. J. has gone to the ends of the earth, it seems, to find the perfect pieces, draperies, and curios. Even the names of the guest rooms, such as Chantilly, Wedgwood, Chelsea, and Greenbriar, were thoughtfully chosen and each unit is decorated just as its name suggests. Each room has its own bathroom, and most have fireplaces. P. J. herself is a gracious host who will look after your every need and cook up a breakfast that could probably keep you going for an entire week. To get here, you'll have to look carefully for the modest, hand-painted sign out front; when you arrive, you'll be treated to freshly baked goodies and a cup of hot tea or lemonade. No smoking.

INEXPENSIVE

Sun & the Moon Bed & Breakfast. 1037 N. Rampart St., New Orleans, LA 70116. ☎ **504/529-4652.** 2 rms. A/C TV MINIBAR. $75 double. Rate includes continental breakfast. No credit cards. Parking available.

Kelly and Taina Mechling, the proprietors of this cozy little bed-and-breakfast, have charmingly furnished and decorated two rooms in Southwest style. Both of the rooms have good-sized, comfortable sleeping and sitting areas. The bathrooms are clean and fully equipped. Each guest room has a minirefrigerator and a separate entrance, which creates a nice sense of privacy. Continental breakfast can be served in your room or on the deck. Maid service is daily.

GUEST HOUSES JUST OUTSIDE THE FRENCH QUARTER
VERY EXPENSIVE

✪ **Melrose Mansion.** 937 Esplanade Ave., New Orleans, LA 70116. ☎ **504/ 944-2255.** Fax 504/945-1794. 8 rms. A/C MINIBAR TV TEL. $225–$250 double; $325–$425 suite. AE, DISC, MC, V. Free parking.

The Melrose Mansion is one of the most splendid guest houses in the city; if you choose to stay here, you will be met at the airport by a chauffeured stretch limousine, which will whisk you to this guest house on the outer limits of the French Quarter. Rosemary and Melvin Jones have lovingly restored this three-story 1884 Victorian mansion. Guest rooms are furnished with marvelous antiques. The mansion's elegant drawing room is the focal point for gatherings for afternoon tea or wine and cheese. Breakfast comes with silver coffee service, beautiful china and crystal, fresh-baked muffins, and fresh fruit and can be served in your room, on the balcony, or at poolside. Rosemary and Melvin are always on hand; there is a wonderfully hospitable butler; and a staff member is always available during the day to make sure that you've got everything you could possibly need.

EXPENSIVE

✪ **The House on Bayou Road.** 2275 Bayou Rd. (just off Esplanade Ave.), New Orleans, LA 70119. ☎ **504/949-7711.** 4 rms, 2 cottages. A/C TEL. $145–$225 double. Rates include breakfast. MC, V. Free parking.

If you want to stay in a rural plantation setting, but still want to be near the French Quarter, The House on Bayou Road might be just the place for you. This intimate Creole plantation home, built in the late 1700s for a colonial Spanish diplomat, has been lovingly restored by owner Cynthia Reeves. As you enter the antique-filled double parlor you'll feel like you're stepping back in time. The individually decorated rooms have a light, airy quality. The large cottage, which is completely separate from the main house, has three rooms that can be rented separately or as a whole. It's perfect for a large family. The small Creole cottage, located next door to the large

New Orleans Accommodations

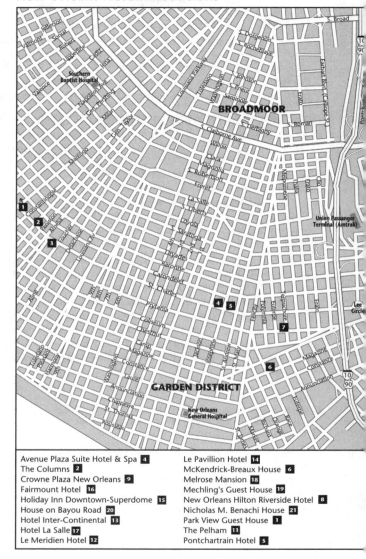

Avenue Plaza Suite Hotel & Spa 4
The Columns 2
Crowne Plaza New Orleans 9
Fairmount Hotel 16
Holiday Inn Downtown-Superdome 15
House on Bayou Road 20
Hotel Inter-Continental 13
Hotel La Salle 17
Le Meridien Hotel 12

Le Pavillion Hotel 14
McKendrick-Breaux House 6
Melrose Mansion 18
Mechling's Guest House 19
New Orleans Hilton Riverside Hotel 8
Nicholas M. Benachi House 21
Park View Guest House 1
The Pelham 11
Pontchartrain Hotel 5

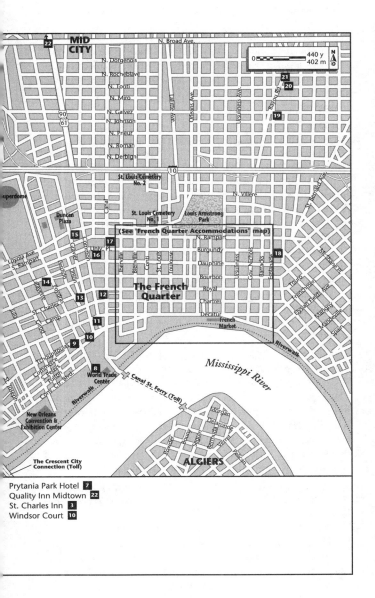

Prytania Park Hotel **7**
Quality Inn Midtown **22**
St. Charles Inn **3**
Windsor Court **10**

cottage, is a great romantic getaway spot. The grounds are beautifully manicured; you can sit either outside on the patio or in the screened-in porch, and there's a swimming pool. In the morning guests are treated to a full plantation-style breakfast, and during the day and in the evening there is access to a minirefrigerator filled with beverages.

MODERATE

The Dufour-Baldwin House. 1707 Esplanade Ave., New Orleans, LA 70116. ☎ **504/945-1503.** 6 rms. A/C TV TEL. $75–$100 double. Weekly discounts available. AE, MC, V. Free parking.

In 1989 Rick Normand and Elizabeth Williams bought this Italianate/late Greek Revival mansion, built in 1859 for Louisiana Senator Cyprien Dufour, and they continue to work at restoring it to its former glory. They're making every effort to find its original furnishings. If you're interested in the process of historic renovation, the Dufour-Baldwin House might be a good choice for you as the front part of the house is still undergoing major work. Not to worry, though: The guest rooms have been completely renovated and they are in a separate wing of the building. All have private entrances and are furnished with antiques. Some have lovely iron beds, local art hangs on the walls, and each room is stocked with a selection of books about the area.

Mechling's Guest House. 2023 Esplanade Ave., New Orleans, LA 70116. ☎ **800/725-4131** or 504/943-4131. Fax 504/944-0956. 5 rms. A/C. $95–$155 double. Rates include full breakfast. AE, MC, V. Free parking.

The guest rooms are on the first floor of this 1860s mansion and retain as many of the original fixtures, windows, and woodwork as could be salvaged. The owners are still working on different parts of the property, including the second floor of the main house and the slave quarters in back. The guest rooms are quite large, most have fireplaces, and all are unique and beautifully decorated.

Nicolas M. Benachi House. 2257 Bayou Rd., New Orleans, LA 70119. ☎ **800/308-7040** or 504/525-7040. 4 rms. A/C TEL. $85–$130 double. Free parking.

This lovely bed-and-breakfast was originally constructed in 1858. Jim Derbes, a lawyer and university instructor, is the fourth owner of the house, and it was under his loving care that it was restored to its current condition. Furnishings in the downstairs public rooms are of the Victorian, rococo revival, Gothic, classical, and Empire styles. Each guest room has a ceiling fan and is furnished with antique and reproduction pieces. Televisions are available on request, and smoking is allowed outdoors only. The Nicolas M. Benachi House has been designated a landmark by the Orleans Parish Landmarks Commission and the Historic Districts Landmarks Commission (from whom Mr. Derbes received the 1985 Honor Award for restoration).

APARTMENTS

Bourgoyne Guest House. 839 Bourbon St., New Orleans, LA 70116. ☎ **504/525-3983** or 504/524-3621. 5 apts. A/C TEL. Studios $77 double; Blue Suite $100 double, $125 triple, $140 quad; Green Suite $110 double, $135 triple, $160 quad. MC, V. Pay parking nearby.

If you're on a budget, the Bourgoyne is a good place to set up home during your stay in New Orleans. Behind the front gate and through the stone carriageway is a quaint courtyard. Each studio room has a fully equipped kitchenette, a bathroom, and a double bed. The studios (and bathrooms) are small and a bit outdated, but functional. The larger apartments, or suites, have kitchens, sitting areas, TVs, and room to sleep three or four. Don't worry about the noise level in the larger apartments as the guest house is far enough up Bourbon Street to be unaffected by the sounds of an average day or night. However, if you're planning to stay in the studio rooms and you're a light sleeper you'll do well to find a room elsewhere.

Napoleon House. 500 Chartres St., New Orleans, LA 70130. ☎ **504/524-9752.** 1 apt. A/C TV TEL. $125–$250. Weekly and monthly rentals are available. AE, DISC, MC, V. No parking available.

If you'd like to experience French Quarter living as a temporary local, I can't think of a better place to do it than in the one apartment that Sal Impastato, owner of the historic Napoleon House, has made available. The three-room upstairs apartment, with two balconies, was the longtime residence of his uncle, and its furnishings are what might be called "New Orleans homey"—several antique pieces intermingle happily with rather well-worn furnishings of indeterminate age but definite comfort. The apartment is right in the heart of the Quarter, with one of the city's best pubs and light-meal restaurants downstairs.

3 Outside the French Quarter

You will find a wide price range of hotels and motels outside the French Quarter, whether you wish to be near the universities, in the Central Business District, or on the outskirts of town.

For those of you who prefer the predictability of a chain hotel, there's a Marriott at 555 Canal St. (☎ **800/228-9290** or 504/581-1000) and a **Hyatt** at 500 Poydras Plaza (☎ **504/561-1234**).

VERY EXPENSIVE

✪ **Fairmont Hotel.** At University Place, 123 Baronne St., New Orleans, LA 70140. ☎ **800/527-4727** or 504/529-7111. 672 rms, 60 suites. A/C TV TEL. $185–$230 double. Extra person $25. AE, DC, DISC, MC, V. Parking $10.

New Orleanians still sometimes think of it as the Roosevelt, and today's Fairmont Hotel upholds the tradition of elegance left by its predecessor. There's the feel of luxury from the moment you enter the magnificent, newly renovated marble and gilded-columned lobby. The rooms are spacious and have high ceilings. Beds are luxuriously outfitted with the finest all-cotton sheets, down pillows, and comforters, and bathroom amenities are custom made for the hotel. For the business traveler, the Fairmont offers in-room computer hookups and fax machines in the suites. In short, the Fairmont is a "grand hotel" in the old manner that offers midtown convenience as a bonus.

Dining/Entertainment: For many years, the sophisticated Blue Room presented headliner entertainers—perhaps you remember those old radio broadcasts "from the Blue Room of the Hotel Roosevelt in downtown New Orleans." Despite restorations, the lovely blue-and-gold decor and French period furnishings have changed very little over the years. These days, the Blue Room is used for private functions only, except for Sunday, when there's a sumptuous brunch. An addition is Bailey's, a casual bistro-style eatery that serves breakfast, lunch, and dinner daily. For fine dining, there's the romantic Sazerac Restaurant.

Services: 24-hour room service, twice-daily maid service, concierge, baby-sitting, activities desk, valet/laundry service.

Facilities: Rooftop health club, pool, tennis courts, beauty shop, business center, gift shop, newsstand, currency exchange.

✪ **Hotel Inter-Continental.** 444 St. Charles Ave., New Orleans, LA 70130. ☎ **800/327-0200** or 504/525-5566. 480 rms, 32 suites. A/C MINIBAR TV TEL. $210–$240 double; $350–$1,700 suite. AE, CB, DC, DISC, MC, V. Valet parking $12.

The Hotel Inter-Continental rises in red granite splendor in the heart of the Central Business District, within walking distance of the French Quarter and the Mississippi River attractions. Its luxurious rooms and suites feature writing desks, separate conversation/dressing areas, minibars, built-in hair dryers, and telephones and

TVs in the bathrooms. The furnishings in both the guest rooms and the public areas are a blend of classic and contemporary styling.

The Governor's Floor (the 14th) is reminiscent of Louisiana's romantic past, and the suites feature period antiques, reproductions, artifacts, and decorations that represent the six heads of state for whom the rooms are named. All the rooms on this floor are decorated individually in blue and cream. The floor has a VIP lounge, which entitles guests to a complimentary continental breakfast and evening cocktails. The Governor's Lounge is stocked with popular periodicals.

Dining/Entertainment: The large marble lobby showcases a cocktail lounge, gourmet meals are served in the Veranda Restaurant (see Chapter 5 for a full listing), and Pete's Pub, on the first floor, serves lunch daily.

Services: 24-hour room service, laundry and valet service, shoe-shine service.

Facilities: Health club and pool, barber shop and beauty salon, gift shop, business center.

Le Meridien Hotel. 614 Canal St., New Orleans, LA 70130. ☎ **504/525-6500.** 494 rms. A/C MINIBAR TV TEL. $180–$260 double; $500–$1,500 suite. AE, CB, DISC, MC, V. Valet parking $12.

The Le Meridien Hotel is one of the city's most dramatic hotels, with lots of marble and a spectacular indoor waterfall. All rooms have multiple-line telephones and a desk and sitting area. Accommodations here are either king- or twin-bedded and are decorated in pleasant neutral tones. There is a complete health club on the premises, and rooms for non-smokers are available. Le Meridien Hotel is an excellent place for viewing Mardi Gras festivities.

Dining/Entertainment: La Gauloise is the hotel's Parisian-style bistro. The Jazz Meridien Club is the hotel's jazz lobby bar and it features entertainment Monday through Saturday.

Services: 24-hour concierge, 24-hour room service, laundry service, baby-sitting, complimentary shoe shine, nightly turndown, business center.

Facilities: Health club, sauna, heated outdoor pool, massage and aerobics, beauty salon, gift shop, jewelry store, art gallery.

Pontchartrain Hotel. 2031 St. Charles Ave., New Orleans, LA 70140. ☎ **800/777-6193** or 504/524-0581. Fax 504/529-1165. 102 rms. A/C TV TEL. $95–$380 based on single occupancy. Extra person $25. Seasonal packages and special promotional rates available. AE, CB, DC, DISC, MC, V. Parking $10 per night.

Named in honor of comte de Pontchartrain from the court of Louis XVI, the elegant Pontchartrain Hotel is located in the Garden District on the St. Charles streetcar line, making it easily accessible from the French Quarter. This landmark hotel (erected in 1927) is a grand structure built in a Moorish architectural style, and the rooms are beautifully furnished. In fact, many original furnishings and antiques are still found in the guest rooms. The service will make you feel pampered within minutes of your arrival—the staff is accustomed to treating guests well because the hotel is a favorite of dignitaries, celebrities, and even royalty. Anne Rice set part of her novel *The Witching Hour* in the hotel and its cafe. Everything in this New Orleans institution is in the continental tradition at its finest.

Dining/Entertainment: The gourmet cuisine of the Caribbean Room (see Chapter 5) is notable. Special low-salt, low-cholesterol menus are available on request. You can have breakfast in Café Pontchartrain and stop for a drink in the Bayou Bar.

Services: 24-hour room service, complimentary shoe shine, complimentary newspaper, nightly turndown service.

✪ **Windsor Court.** 300 Gravier St., New Orleans, LA 70140. ☎ **800/ 262-2662** or 504/523-6000. Fax 504/596-4513. 319 rms and suites. A/C TV TEL. $235–$320 standard guest room; $310–$405 junior suite; $390–$580 full suite; $590–$990 two-bedroom suite. Children under 12 free in parents' room. AE, CB, DC, MC, V. Valet parking $15.

The centrally located, 24-story Windsor Court, with its pink granite facade, is one of the city's loveliest hotels. A proper English tea is served in Le Salon (in the first-floor lobby), accompanied by live chamber music. Two corridors are minigalleries displaying original 17th-, 18th-, and 19th-century works of art. Italian marble and antique furnishings distinguish public spaces. Both suites and standard guest rooms are exceptionally spacious and beautifully furnished with four-poster and canopy beds. Each suite is individually decorated and features large bay windows or a private balcony overlooking the river or the city, a private foyer, a large living room, a bedroom entered through French doors, a marble bath, separate his-and-her dressing rooms, and a "petite kitchen." Most of the rooms here are suites.

Dining/Entertainment: The Polo Club Lounge has the ambience of a private English club; the Grill Room Restaurant serves breakfast, brunch, lunch, and dinner; Le Salon, the lobby lounge, serves afternoon tea, cocktails, and sweets and has chamber music and piano music during the day and evening.

Services: 24-hour suite service (much more than your average room service), full concierge service.

Facilities: Among the guest facilities are a health club with a resort-size pool, sauna, and steam room. Numerous conveniences are available for business travelers, who might want to conduct conferences in the privacy of their own suites or in the specially planned meeting spaces.

EXPENSIVE

Crowne Plaza New Orleans. 300 Poydras St., New Orleans, LA 70130. ☎ **504/525-9444.** 441 rms. A/C TV TEL. $200 double; $375–$675 suite. AE, CB, DC, DISC, MC, V. Valet parking $12; self-parking $8.50

The Crowne Plaza New Orleans has recently renovated guest units, suites, an Executive Floor, and a restaurant, deli, and lounge. It's an attractive hotel that includes among its many amenities a pool with poolside beverage service, an exercise room, and free in-room movies. Suites and the 22 rooms on the luxury-level Executive Floor come with a complimentary continental breakfast and refreshments, refrigerators, and a private cocktail lounge.

New Orleans Hilton Riverside Hotel. 2 Poydras St., New Orleans, LA 70140. ☎ **800/445-8667** or 504/561-0500. Fax 504/568-1721. 1,602 rms. A/C MINIBAR TV TEL. $275–$295 double; $580–$1,870 suite. Special packages available. AE, CB, DC, DISC, JCB, MC, V. Parking $12 for 24 hours.

The New Orleans Hilton Riverside Hotel, at the Mississippi River, has perhaps more than any other new hotel integrated itself successfully into the lifestyle of the city. Located in what some are calling the "River Quarter," the Hilton sits right at the riverfront, adjacent to the World Trade Center of New Orleans and the New Orleans Convention Center, yet it somehow manages to avoid the sterile impersonality projected by so many large hotels. There are nice touches, such as warm colors, Italian oak and mahogany paneling, and deep-pile carpeting. The 90-foot, nine-story, multilevel atrium creates a feeling of space without that rattle-around boxiness. Guest rooms are spacious, and most have fabulous views of the river or the city; all are furnished in a country French manner, using muted colors and draperies keyed to the etched toile of the wall coverings.

Dining/Entertainment: The atrium is broken up into attractive centers, such as the English Bar, Le Café Bromeliad, and the French Garden Bar. There are in fact seven restaurants and lounges within the complex. Pete Fountain moved his jazz club from the Quarter to a third-floor replica here. A relatively new addition to the Hilton is the Flamingo Casino: 20,000 square feet of gambling space on board a riverboat.

Services: 24-hour room service, concierge service, laundry/valet/pressing service, airport transportation, shoe-shine service.

Facilities: Guests are eligible for membership in the hotel's Rivercenter Racquet and Health Club, which includes outdoor and indoor tennis courts, squash and racquetball courts, a rooftop jogging track, aerobics classes, tanning beds, massage, a hair salon, and a golf studio.

The Pelham. 444 Common St., New Orleans, LA 70130. ☎ **800/659-5621** or 504/522-4444. Fax 504/539-9010. 60 rms, 2 suites. A/C TV TEL. $149–$229 double. AE, DC, DISC, MC, V. Parking $12 a day.

If you're not interested in staying right in the French Quarter, want more independence than is offered at a bed-and-breakfast, and would like to be as far away from conventioneers as possible, the recently opened Pelham is an excellent choice. The small hotel, located in a beautifully renovated building that dates from the late 1800s, is cozy and attractively decorated. Centrally located rooms are generally less bright than those on the exterior of the building, but I had no complaints with any of them.

MODERATE

Avenue Plaza Suite Hotel & Spa. 2111 St. Charles Ave., New Orleans, LA 70130. ☎ **800/535-9575** or 504/566-1212. Fax 504/525-6899. 250 rms. A/C TV TEL. $89–$199 double. AE, DC, DISC, MC, V. Parking $8.

Located in the picturesque Garden District on the historic St. Charles Avenue streetcar line, the Avenue Plaza Suite Hotel & Spa features, after a $7 million renovation, completely refurbished suites and public spaces. Each suite in this 18th-century antebellum home has a kitchenette and is attractively furnished. Special amenities are the Mackie Shilstone Pro Spa, Health Club, and Salon. There is a rooftop sundeck and a courtyard swimming pool. A cafe and lounge are located on the premises.

The Columns. 3811 St. Charles Ave., New Orleans, LA 70115. ☎ **504/899-9308.** 19 rms (9 with bath). A/C TEL. $75–$175 double. Rates include continental breakfast. AE, MC, V. Parking available on the street.

The Columns, built in 1883 by Simon Hernsheim, a wealthy tobacco merchant, is one of the greatest examples of a late 19th-century Louisiana residence. You'll be impressed by the grand, columned entrance. Its architectural style is Italianate, or pre–Queen Anne, and most of the original interior features still exist. The wide mahogany staircase is truly awesome, as is the stained-glass, domed skylight above it. The furnishings, however, are becoming a bit run down. There's a lot more charm and character than elegance here these days, but it's worth looking into because of the reasonable rates and the clean and comfortable rooms. All the rooms and furnishings are different—some rooms have wood sleigh beds, while others have double beds with intricately carved head- and footboards. Many have couches and chairs, while some are much too small to accommodate such furnishings. The rooms with baths have claw-foot tubs, and the rooms without baths come equipped with sinks. The Columns was the setting of Louis Malle's film *Pretty Baby* and is listed in the National Register of Historic Places. Albertine's Tea Room, is open for lunch, dinner, and Sunday brunch, and the Victorian lounge is open for evening cocktails.

Holiday Inn Downtown-Superdome. 330 Loyola Ave., New Orleans, LA 70112. ☎ **504/581-1600.** Fax 504/522-0073. 297 rms. A/C TV TEL. $94–$209 double; $350 suite. Extra person $15. Children 19 and under free in parents' room. AE, CB, DC, DISC, JCB, MC, V. Parking $10.

The 18-story Holiday Inn Downtown-Superdome is centrally located, with easy access to New Orleans's business and financial centers, as well as the Louisiana Superdome and the French Quarter. Each room has a balcony and city view, and the hotel has a collection of jazz scene murals available for public viewing. In addition, the dining room here holds an interesting collection of New Orleans streetcar paintings. The Mardi Gras Lounge offers cocktails and after-dinner drinks nightly. There is a rooftop heated pool.

⑤ Le Pavillon Hotel. 833 Poydras St., New Orleans, LA 70140. ☎ **800/535-9095** or 504/581-3111. Fax 504/522-5543. 220 rms, 7 suites. A/C TV TEL. From $109 double; from $395 suite. AE. Parking available.

Established in 1907, Le Pavillon was the first hotel in New Orleans to have elevators and is a member of the Historic Hotels of America. The lobby is stunning, with high ceilings, grand columns, plush furnishings, Oriental rugs, detailed woodwork, and 11 crystal chandeliers imported from Czechoslovakia. Each hall features massive Louisiana antiques and has 14 original paintings from the hotel's fine-arts collection. The standard guest rooms are similar in terms of furnishings but differ in size by virtue of the hotel's original floor plan, which for the most part has remained intact. The Pavillon also has some fine suites for very reasonable rates. And guests are treated to complimentary peanut-butter-and-jelly sandwiches and a glass of milk each evening in the lobby.

Dining/Entertainment: The Gold Room, the hotel's large dining room, is open for breakfast, lunch, and dinner daily. A beautiful room, it has a working fireplace, which makes for a cozy atmosphere. The hotel lounge is the Gallery, which serves complimentary hors d'oeuvres Monday to Friday from 4 to 7pm.

Services: 24-hour room service, complimentary shoe shine, full concierge service.

Facilities: Heated rooftop pool, fitness center, and whirlpool spa.

Prytania Park Hotel. 1519 Terpsichore St., New Orleans, LA 70130. ☎ **800/862-1984** or 504/524-0427. Fax 504/522-2977. 62 rms. A/C MINIBAR TV TEL. $109 double; $119 suite. Rates include continental breakfast. Seasonal rates are available. Extra person $10. Children under 12 free. Special packages available. AE, CB, DC, DISC, MC, V. Free parking.

Centrally located in the historic Garden District, the Prytania Park is a charming hotel run with the same personal attention as a guest house. The Victorian building, which dates from 1834, is beautifully restored and furnished in period, hand-carved English pine. The Victorian town house rooms also have high ceilings and exposed brick walls. The 49 rooms in the modern addition retain the New Orleans architectural ambience, but have more contemporary furnishings than the 13 rooms in the original part of the hotel; they open onto landscaped courtyards and come with microwave ovens and refrigerators. The St. Charles Avenue streetcar line is half a block away, providing quick and easy access to the French Quarter (15 blocks away) and all the major attractions. And the hotel is situated in the heart of the uptown restaurant district; cuisine and prices here vary widely enough to fit all kinds of gastronomic yearnings and budgets.

INEXPENSIVE

Hotel La Salle. 1113 Canal St., New Orleans, LA 70112. ☎ **800/521-9450** in the U.S. or 504/523-5831. Fax 504/525-2531. 57 rms (42 with bath). A/C TV TEL. $45 double without bath; $64 double with bath. Children under 12 free in parents' room. AE, DC, DISC, JCB, MC, V. Free parking.

You'll find convenience and comfort at budget prices only half a block outside the French Quarter at the Hotel La Salle. The no-frills rooms are plainly furnished, clean, and comfortable and come with or without private bath. There's an old-fashioned air to the small lobby with its high ceilings, overhead fans, carved Austrian wall clock, and old-time wooden reception desk. Free coffee is always available in the lobby, and guests receive a complimentary newspaper daily. This is a favorite with European visitors who appreciate bathroom-down-the-hall savings.

Quality Inn Midtown. 3900 Tulane Ave., New Orleans, LA 70119. ☎ **800/ 486-5541** or 504/486-5541. Fax 504/488-7440. 102 rms. A/C TV TEL. $69– $300 double; $180–$300 suite. Extra person $10–$20. AE, DC, DISC, MC, V. Free parking.

The Quality Inn Midtown is located only about five minutes from the Central Business District. All the rooms have balconies; many face the courtyard, are spacious, and have double beds. The hotel's French Quarter–style courtyard features a swimming pool and Jacuzzi. There is free shuttle service available daily to the French Quarter and convention center. Guests also have use of coin-operated laundry facilities and movies are free. A restaurant and lounge are open daily.

St. Charles Inn. 3636 St. Charles Ave., New Orleans, LA 70115. ☎ **800/ 489-9908** or 504/899-8888. Fax 504/899-8892. 40 rms. A/C TV TEL. $75 double. Rate includes continental breakfast. AE, DC, DISC, MC, V. Parking $3 outdoors.

The St. Charles Inn is only five minutes away from Tulane and Loyola universities and 10 minutes from the French Quarter or Louisiana Superdome via the trolley. Each room has either two double beds or a king-size bed. Facilities here include a lounge and a restaurant, and there are extras like continental breakfast served in your room and complimentary morning newspaper.

GUEST HOUSES

If you're in New Orleans to visit Tulane University, Loyola University, or Newcomb College, or if you just want to stay out of the hustle and bustle of downtown, you'll want to know about these conveniently located guest houses.

⑤ The McKendrick-Breaux House. 1474 Magazine St., New Orleans, LA 70130. ☎ **504/586-1700.** 5 rms. A/C TV TEL. $90–$135 double. Rates include breakfast. Limited free off-street parking is available.

You'd be hard pressed to find more gracious hosts than Lisa and Eddie Breaux, owners of the McKendrick-Breaux House. The young couple saved the two houses on their property from ultimate destruction. Breakfast is served each morning in the downstairs parlor and adjoining dining room. Rooms are located both in the main house and the building directly across the quiet courtyard (which was once the site of a bar). All rooms are extremely spacious and are furnished with antiques and family collectibles. Bathrooms are large as well. The ones in the main house have beautiful claw-foot tubs, while those in the building opposite are huge and have modern fixtures. Fresh flowers greet you on arrival, and Lisa and Eddie will supply your room with a bucket of ice every evening.

Note: At press time there were plans in the works to add two more rooms to the upper floor.

Park View Guest House. 7004 St. Charles Ave., New Orleans, LA 70118. ☎ **504/861-7564.** 23 rms (17 with bath). A/C TEL. $75–$80 double without bath, $80–$90 double with bath. Rates include continental breakfast. Extra person $10. AE, MC, V. On-street parking.

On the far edge of Audubon Park is the Park View Guest House, a rambling Victorian structure built in 1884 as a hotel for the Cotton Exposition. It's listed on the National Register of Historic Places. A front door that sparkles with etched-glass panels admits you to the wide central hall with gleaming crystal chandeliers. A lovely stained-glass window is the focal point of the large lounge furnished with comfortable sofas and chairs. All the rooms are furnished in antiques and reflect an old-fashioned comfort that's hard to resist; some have balconies. There's a large dining room, with windows overlooking the park, where a continental breakfast is served daily. All guests have the use of a refrigerator and ice machine anytime.

AIRPORT HOTELS

Downtown New Orleans is only a 15-minute drive from the airport (located in nearby Kenner), so even if you're only going to be in town overnight you can still take a room in one of the hotels mentioned above without inconveniencing yourself.

However, if you'd rather just stay near the airport, there are several hotels from which to choose. If you want to spend a night in Kenner in style, make a reservation at the **New Orleans Airport Hilton,** located at 901 Airline Hwy., Kenner, LA 70062 (☎ **800/ 445-8667** or 504/469-5000). The 312-room Hilton features a lighted tennis court, fitness center, putting green, gift shop, restaurant, and business center. **The Holiday Inn New Orleans— Airport,** 2929 Williams Blvd., Kenner, LA 70062 (☎ **800/ 465-4329** or 504/467-5611), is a less-expensive alternative. It also has a restaurant, exercise room, pool, and sauna. Both hotels offer airport transfer.

5

Dining

*N*ew and relatively recent openings of particular note include Gabrielle, on Esplanade Avenue, and the Pelican Club, Nola, and Bacco (all in the French Quarter). I personally guarantee you a good time if you try any one of those four. Of course, there may be some even newer ones opened by the time you get there, so ask at your hotel, or ask a local (no one knows food like a native New Orleanian!).

Good eating in New Orleans is by no means confined to the French Quarter—you'll find it all over town. I've defined neighborhoods in this chapter in rather broad terms: "downtown" (remember, that's *downriver* from Canal Street) is outside the French Quarter but on the same side of Canal Street; the Central Business District is roughly the area upriver from Canal, extending to the elevated expressway (U.S. 90); "uptown" includes everything upriver from Canal and as far as Carrollton toward the lake, including the Garden District; Metairie is New Orleans's next-door neighbor in Jefferson Parish; the "lake," of course, means the area along the shores of Lake Pontchartrain.

1 Best Bets

- **Best Spot for a Business Lunch: Mr. B's Bistro & Bar,** 201 Royal St. (☎ **504/523-2078**), is packed with locals during the lunch hour. The atmosphere is casual but classic, and wood-and-glass partitions break up the otherwise large dining room, keeping noise levels low.
- **Best Wine List:** The wine cellar at **Brennan's,** 417 Royal St. (☎ **504/525-9711**), is virtually unsurpassed in New Orleans. There's a good selection of less-expensive California wines, some moderately priced French selections, as well as some more expensive labels and a lovely selection of dessert wines.
- **Best for Kids:** I haven't yet met a kid who didn't go wild for hot chocolate and beignets, best enjoyed at **Café du Monde,** in the French Market, 813 Decatur (☎ **504/581-2914**). They

especially love getting powdered sugar all over their faces. In addition, street performers around the cafe, especially the ones that make animal balloons and hats, are top entertainment for children.

- **Best French Cuisine:** The city's first French restaurant, **Louis XVI,** 829 Toulouse St. (☎ **504/581-7000**), remains its best. Plush surroundings and tableside preparations complete the dining experience.

- **Best Cajun:** It may have a fast-food atmosphere, but **Copeland's,** 4339 St. Charles Ave. (☎ **504/897-2325**), is known citywide for producing the best Cajun dishes around. Chef George Rhode IV has an unwavering commitment to freshness—he makes his sauces and stocks from scratch—yet still manages to turn out an extraordinary variety of dishes every night.

- **Best Creole:** When the **Praline Connection,** 542 Frenchmen St. (☎ **504/943-3934**), came on the scene a couple of years back it quickly became the city's favorite place for good Creole cooking—beans and rice, jambalaya, and crawfish étouffée.

- **Best Desserts:** There are a number of places in New Orleans where you'll find outstanding desserts, but **Commander's Palace,** 1403 Washington Ave. (☎ **504/899-8221**), has them all beat. Their repertoire is unsurpassed: Creole bread pudding, Bananas Foster cheese cake, anything flaming, anything chocolate, and always, lemon crepes.

- **Best Italian: Bacco,** 310 Chartres St. (☎ **504/522-2426**), brainchild of the Brennan family, took New Orleans by storm a couple of years ago and is still going strong. The emphasis is on tradition, but a Creole twist maintains the creative spirit expected of the Brennans. Dishes like penne with tomatoes and roasted eggplant and crawfish ravioli are among the best I've had.

- **Best New American:** When it comes to American food there's not a doubt in my mind (or in the minds of most New Orleanians) that **Emeril's,** 800 Tchoupitoulas St. (☎ **504/528-9393**), sets the pace in this town. As a base for his creations, nationally renowned chef Emeril Legasse uses Creole preparations and then gives them an enormous kick into the nineties with the addition of modern American touches. What he ends up with is some of the freshest (he makes most everything, from ketchup to cheese, himself) and most innovative dishes in New Orleans.

- **Best Burgers:** Ask anyone in town where to get the best hamburger and they'll all tell you to head straight for **Port of Call,** 838 Esplanade Ave. (☎ **504/523-0120**), an appropriately casual hole in the wall at the edge of the French Quarter. I know people who won't leave town until they've downed one of Port of Call's giant burgers and enormous baked potatoes (always done to perfection).

- **Best Steaks:** Don't be turned off by the fact that **Ruth's Chris Steakhouse,** 711 N. Broad St. (☎ **504/486-0810**), is part of a chain. Chefs there serve up the best beef around. You'll be hard pressed to find better anywhere else.
- **Best Outdoor Dining:** My personal favorite is the beautiful, quiet, and fairly secluded courtyard at **Bayona,** 430 Dauphine St. (☎ **504/525-4455**). It's particularly lovely on a spring afternoon at lunch, and chef Susan Spicer's innovative international cuisine is hard to beat.
- **Best Afternoon Tea:** Everyone loves spending an afternoon in **Le Salon** at the Windsor Court hotel, 300 Gravier St. (☎ **504/523-6000**), enjoying tea, scones, a little chamber music, and the Windsor's ultra-elegant surroundings.
- **Best Picnic Fare:** My personal favorite for picnic fare is **Central Grocery** (located on Decatur Street). Pick up a muffaletta sandwich from this wonderful Italian delicatessen and specialty food shop.
- **Best Views:** At **Bella Luna,** 914 N. Peters (☎ **504/529-1583**), you'll not only get great Italian food, but you'll be treated to a moonlight view of the Mississippi.

2 Restaurants by Cuisine

AMERICAN & NEW AMERICAN

Bluebird Cafe (Central Business District, *I*)

Cafe Sbisa (French Quarter, *E*)

Emeril's (Central Business District, *E*)

G&E Courtyard Grill (French Quarter, *M*)

Mike's on the Avenue (Uptown, *E*)

Napoleon House (French Quarter, *I*)

Nola (French Quarter, *E*)

Pelican Club (French Quarter, *E*)

Rémoulade (French Quarter, *M*)

CAFES

Café du Monde (French Quarter, *I*)

New Orleans Coffee and Concierge (French Quarter, *I*)

Royal Blend Coffee and Tea House (French Quarter, *I*)

St. Ann's Cafe and Deli (French Quarter, *I*)

Key to Abbreviations: *E*=Expensive; *I*=Inexpensive ; *M*=Moderate; *VE*=Very Expensive

CAJUN

Bon Ton Café (Central
Business District, *M*)
Bozo's (Metairie, *I*)
Brigtsen's (Uptown, *E*)
Copeland's (Uptown, *M*)
Ernst's Café (Central
Business District, *I*)
K-Paul's Louisiana Kitchen
(French Quarter, *E*)
Olde N'Awlins Cookery
(French Quarter, *M*)
Père Antoine Restaurant
(French Quarter, *I*)
Petunia's (French Quarter, *I*)

COFFEE SHOPS

Bailey's (Central Business
District, *M*)

COFFEE, TEA & SWEETS

Angelo Brocato's Ice Cream
and Confectionery
(French Quarter, *I*)
Café du Monde (French
Quarter, *I*)
La Madeleine (French
Quarter, *I*)
La Marquise (French
Quarter, *I*)
P. J.'s Coffee and Tea
Company (French
Quarter, *I*)

CONTINENTAL

Sazerac (Uptown, *E*)
The Veranda Restaurant
(Central Business
District, *E*)

CREOLE

Arnaud's (French
Quarter, *E*)
Bacco (French
Quarter, *E*)
Brigtsen's (Uptown, *E*)
Commander's Palace
(Uptown, *E*)
Copeland's (Uptown, *M*)
Court of Two Sisters
(French Quarter, *E*)
Dooky Chase (Down-
town, *M*)
Emeril's (Central Business
District, *E*)
Ernst's Café (Central
Business District, *I*)
Felix's Restaurant and
Oyster Bar (French
Quarter, *I*)
Gumbo Shop (French
Quarter, *M*)
Mother's (Central Business
District, *I*)
Mr. B's Bistro and Bar
(French Quarter, *M*)
Olde N'Awlins Cookery
(French Quarter, *M*)
Palace Café (Central
Business District, *M*)
Père Antoine Restaurant
(French Quarter, *I*)
Petunia's (French
Quarter, *I*)
Praline Connection
(French Quarter, *I*)
Ralph and Kacoo's
(French Quarter, *M*)
Rémoulade (French

Quarter, *M*)
Rita's Olde French Quarter
Restaurant (French
Quarter, *M*)
Royal Café (French
Quarter, *M*)
Sazerac (Uptown, *E*)
Tujague's (French
Quarter, *M*)
Upperline (Uptown, *E*)
The Veranda Restaurant
(Central Business
District, *E*)

ECLECTIC

Bella Luna (French
Quarter, *E*)
Graham's (Central Business
District, *E*)
Upperline (Uptown, *E*)

FRENCH & FRENCH/ CREOLE

Antoine's (French
Quarter, *E*)
Brennan's (French
Quarter, *E*)
Broussard's (French
Quarter, *E*)
Caribbean Room
(Uptown, *E*)
Christian's (Downtown, *M*)
Crozier's Restaurant Français
(Metairie, *M*)
Galatoire's (French
Quarter, *E*)
Louis XVI (French
Quarter, *E*)
Palm Court Café (French
Quarter, *M*)

Peristyle (French
Quarter, *E*)
The Versailles
(Uptown, *E*)

HAMBURGERS

Camellia Grill
(Uptown, *I*)
Port of Call (French
Quarter, *M*)

INTERNATIONAL

Bayona (French Quarter, *E*)
Gabrielle (French
Quarter, *M*)
Gautreau's (Uptown, *M*)
Le Bistro (French
Quarter, *E*)

ITALIAN

Alberto's (French
Quarter, *M*)
Bacco (French Quarter, *E*)
Dipiazza's (French
Quarter, *M*)
Louisiana Pizza Kitchen
(French Quarter, *I*)
Mama Rosa's (French
Quarter, *I*)
Maximo's Italian Grill
(French Quarter, *M*)
Napoleon House (French
Quarter, *I*)
Pascal's Manale (Uptown, *E*)
Peristyle (French Quarter, *E*)
Ristorante Carmelo (French
Quarter, *M*)

LATE NIGHT/24 HOUR

St. Ann's Cafe and Deli
(French Quarter, *I*)

SANDWICHES

Café Maspero (French
  Quarter, *I*)
Camellia Grill
  (Uptown, *I*)
Mother's (Central
  Business District, *I*)
Uglesich's Restaurant
  and Bar (Central
  Business District, *I*)

SEAFOOD

Acme Oyster House (French
  Quarter, *I*)
Bozo's (Metairie, *I*)
Café Maspero (French
  Quarter, *I*)
Casamento's (Uptown, *M*)
Felix's Restaurant and
  Oyster Bar (French
  Quarter, *I*)
Kabby's Seafood Restaurant
  (Central Business
  District, *M*)

Mike Anderson's Seafood
  (French Quarter, *M*)
Olde N'Awlins Cookery
  (French Quarter, *M*)
Ralph & Kacoo's (French
  Quarter, *M*)

SEAFOOD/STEAKS

Delmonico Restaurant
  (Uptown, *M*)
Rib Room (French
  Quarter, *E*)
Tavern on the Park
  (Uptown, *M*)

SOUL FOOD

Dooky Chase (Down-
  town, *M*)
Praline Connection (French
  Quarter, *I*)

STEAKS

Pascal's Manale (Uptown, *E*)
Ruth's Chris Steak House
  (Downtown, *M*)

<h1 style="background:black;color:white;">3 In the French Quarter</h1>

EXPENSIVE

Antoine's. 713 St. Louis St. ☎ **504/581-4422.** Reservations required. Main courses $14.25–$49. AE, DC, MC, V. Mon–Sat 11:30am–2pm and 5:30–9pm. FRENCH/CREOLE.

Who hasn't heard of Antoine's and dreamed of at least one meal in this legendary restaurant, run by the same family for more than 150 years? Once inside the ironwork-adorned building, you're in a world of white-tile floors and slowly turning antique ceiling fans. Fifteen separate rooms run the gamut from plainness to grandeur.

Choose from such classics as alligator soup and filet de boeuf marchand de vin; or settle for something simpler from a menu that lists more than 150 selections. To accompany your choice you have at your disposal one of the richest wine cellars in America. Baked Alaska is the favorite dessert here.

A few tips: The menu now has English translations. Even with reservations, be prepared for a wait at peak hours. If you want to dine with locals, try for a table in the Annex. Antoine's has added a less pricey lunch menu.

Arnaud's. 813 Bienville St. ☎ **504/523-5433.** Reservations recommended. Main courses $15.50–$39.95. AE, DC, MC, V. Mon–Fri 11:30am–2:30pm; Sun–Thurs 6–10pm, Fri–Sat 6–10:30pm; brunch Sun 10am–2:30pm. CREOLE.

Housed in buildings dating from the 1700s, Arnaud's was opened in 1918 by "Count" Arnaud Cazenave (the fictitious title was bestowed by locals in recognition of his grand manner); after his death in 1948 the old traditions were carried on for many years by his daughter. Then a decline set in that eventually led to the restaurant's desertion by even the most loyal of its wide clientele. But in late 1978 Archie and Jane Casbarian bought it and began an extensive restoration. With its flickering gaslights, dark-wood paneling, original ceiling medallions, and antique ceiling fans, the large dining room exudes a turn-of-the-century air. Tables are laid with classic linen and set with sterling silver, original Arnaud china, and fine crystal. Executive chef Kevin Davis turns out specialties such as trout meunière and a superb crème brûlée, and he constantly creates exciting new dishes. At lunch there's an inexpensive table d'hôte (fixed-price) selection along with an à la carte menu, and on Sunday there's a jazz brunch.

✪ **Bacco.** 310 Chartres St. ☎ **504/522-2426.** Reservations recommended. Main courses $16.50–$21. AE, DC, MC, V. Mon–Sat 7–10am, Sun 8:30–10am; Mon–Sat 11:30am–2:30pm; brunch Sun 10:30am–2:30pm; daily 6–10pm. ITALIAN/CREOLE.

Located next door to the Hotel de la Poste, Bacco is a new addition to the scene. The interior, with pink Italian marble floors, wall and ceiling murals, Venetian chandeliers, and Gothic arches, is stunning. At lunch try the Louisiana crab cakes and fettuccine. Begin your dinner with a Creole-Italian specialty, Bacco shrimp (spicy jumbo gulf shrimp roasted in the wood-burning oven, served in a garlic pepper oil). One of my favorite dinner entrées is the crawfish ravioli (homemade ravioli filled with crawfish tails, onions, sweet peppers, and Creole seasonings tossed in a sun-dried tomato pesto sauce). There are daily specials as well. For dessert try the frozen cappuccino (homemade espresso ice served with Grand Marnier double cream and a biscotti).

✪ **Bayona.** 430 Dauphine St. ☎ **504/525-4455.** Reservations required at dinner; recommended at lunch. Main courses $9–$20. AE, CB, DC, DISC, MC, V. Mon–Fri 11:30am–2pm; Mon–Thurs 6–9:30pm, Fri–Sat 6–10:30pm. INTERNATIONAL.

New Orleans Dining

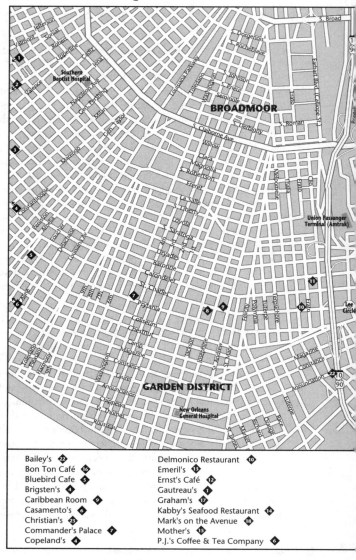

Bailey's ◆②
Bon Ton Café ◆⑯
Bluebird Cafe ◆⑤
Brigsten's ◆④
Caribbean Room ◆⑨
Casamento's ◆⑥
Christian's ◆㉓
Commander's Palace ◆⑦
Copeland's ◆④

Delmonico Restaurant ◆⑩
Emeril's ◆⑬
Ernst's Café ◆⑫
Gautreau's ◆①
Graham's ◆⑰
Kabby's Seafood Restaurant ◆⑭
Mark's on the Avenue ◆⑱
Mother's ◆⑮
P.J.'s Coffee & Tea Company ◆⑥

70

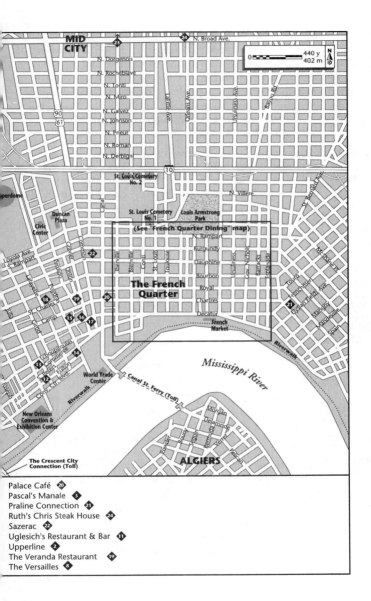

0 ▭▬▬▬ 440 y
         402 m

N

MID
CITY

N. Broad Ave.

N. Dorgenois
N. Rocheblave
N. Tonti
N. Miro
N. Galvez
N. Johnson
N. Prieur
N. Roman
N. Derbigny

La Fitte Ave.
Orleans Ave.
Ursulines Ave.
Bayou Rd.

90
61

10

St. Louis Cemetery
No. 2

N. Villère

St. Bernard Ave.

Superdome

Duncan
Plaza

Civic
Center

Canal

St. Louis Cemetery
No. 1

Louis Armstrong
Park

(See "French Quarter Dining" map)

N. Rampart

Burgundy

Dauphine

Bourbon

Royal

Chartres

Decatur

Iberville
Bienville
Conti
St. Louis
Toulouse

Iberville
Bienville

Ursulines
Gov. Nichols
Barracks
Esplanade

The French
Quarter

Loyola Ave.
S. Rampart

22

Gravier

Common

Poydras

18

19

20

St. Charles

Camp

15 16 17

Tchoupitoulas
Commerce

14

13
Peters
Fulton

12

Conv. Ctr. Blvd.

World Trade
Center

Canal St. Ferry (Toll)

Riverwalk

Mississippi River

Riverwalk

French
Market

21

Touro
Frenchmen
Elysian Fields Ave.
Mandeville
Marigny
Spain

New Orleans
Convention &
Exhibition Center

Morgan

Delaronde

Joseph

The Crescent City
Connection (Toll)

Teche
Bouny
Seguin
Bermuda
Verret
Pelican

ALGIERS

Palace Café ⓴
Pascal's Manale ❸
Praline Connection ㉑
Ruth's Chris Steak House ㉔
Sazerac ㉒
Uglesich's Restaurant & Bar ⓫
Upperline ❷
The Veranda Restaurant ⑲
The Versailles ❽

71

After bringing success to Le Bistro (see below), innovative chef Susan Spicer decided to open a restaurant of her own. The atmosphere in the century-old Creole cottage is convivial and comfortable, yet elegant, but if you'd rather have a quiet open-air dining experience, there are some tables in the courtyard as well. Begin your meal here with the cream of garlic soup (one of Spicer's signature dishes). As a main course, try the Parmesan-crusted rabbit with a lemon-sage sauce. The wine list here is excellent.

✪ **Bella Luna.** 914 N. Peters. ☎ **504/529-1583.** Reservations recommended. Main courses $12–$24. AE, CB, DC, DISC, MC, V. Mon–Sat 6–10:30pm, Sun 6–9:30pm. ECLECTIC/CONTINENTAL.

Though the interior of Bella Luna is reminiscent of an Italian villa, complete with tile floors, the cuisine is not so easy to pin down. Adventurous and creative, German chef Horst Pfeifer turns out delicious appetizers like Southwest duck enchiladas with roasted tomatillo salsa and fresh thyme with unflagging consistency. Main courses might include house-cured pork chop in a New Orleans–style pecan crust with horseradish mashed potatoes and an Abita beer sauce. Pastas also have a place on the menu. The dessert menu changes frequently, but if the chocolate bellini napoleon is on the menu, give it a try.

Brennan's. 417 Royal St. ☎ **504/525-9711.** Reservations recommended. Main courses at dinner $28.50–$35. AE, CB, DC, DISC, JCB, MC, V. Daily 8am–2:30pm and 6–10pm. Closed Christmas. FRENCH/CREOLE.

Brennan's, one of the most famous New Orleans restaurants, occupies a 1795 building. It's been here since 1946 and from the start has won a place in the hearts of residents and visitors alike. Be prepared, however, to wait for breakfast and lunch, even if you have a reservation. It's less crowded at dinner. The lush tropical patio here has to be seen to be believed, and there's a view of it from any table in the downstairs rooms.

Served throughout the day, "Breakfast at Brennan's" has become internationally famous. This is not your typical bacon-and-eggs affair, but breakfast in the tradition of antebellum days in the Quarter. If you really want to do it right, order one of their complete breakfast suggestions. A typical one begins with eggs Sardou (poached eggs atop creamed spinach and artichoke bottoms, served with hollandaise sauce), followed by grillades and grits, sautéed baby veal (served in a spicy Creole sauce with fines herbes and freshly cracked black pepper), and topped off by crepes Fitzgerald (cream cheese–filled crepes with a sauce of crushed strawberries flamed in

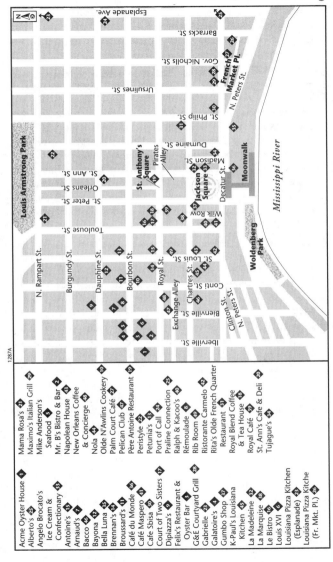

Acme Oyster House 1
Alberto's 23
Angelo Brocato's
  Ice Cream &
  Confectionary 43
Antoine's 7
Arnaud's 7
Bacco 39
Bella Luna 42
Brennan's 18
Broussard's 13
Café Maspero 36
Cafe Sbisa 50
Court of Two Sisters 47
Dipiazza's 9
Felix's Restaurant &
  Oyster Bar 3
G&E Courtyard Grill 2
Gabrielle 32
Galatoire's 4
Gumbo Shop 20
K-Paul's Louisiana
  Kitchen 35
La Madeleine 34
La Marquise 46
Le Bistro 6
Louis XVI 8
Louisiana Pizza Kitchen
  (Esplanade) 43
Louisiana Pizza Kitche
  (Fr. Mkt. Pl.) 26

Mama Rosa's 21
Maximo's Italian Grill 46
Mike Anderson's
  Seafood 5
Mr. B's Bistro & Bar 2
Napolean House 12
New Orleans Coffee
  & Concierge 33
Nola 19
Olde N'Awlins Cookery 40
Palm Court Café 47
Pelican Club 11
Père Antoine Restaurant 19
Peristyle 22
Petunia's 44
Port of Call 24
Praline Connection 23
Ralph & Kacoo's 5
Rémoulade 8
Rib Room 10
Ristorante Carmelo 42
Rita's Olde French Quarter
  Restaurant 31
Royal Blend Coffee
  & Tea House 16
Royal Café 17
St. Ann's Cafe & Deli 38
Tujague's 34

maraschino) and hot chicory coffee. The dinner menu features oysters Rockefeller, followed by specials like steak Diane and shrimp Creole. Desserts include the usual bananas Foster and crepes Fitzgerald, among others.

Broussard's. 819 Conti St. ☎ **504/581-3866.** Reservations required. Main courses $19.50–$32.50. AE, CB, DC, DISC, MC, V. Daily 5:30–10pm. FRENCH/CREOLE.

Broussard's was purchased in 1993 by the Preuss family, and they have breathed new life into this landmark restaurant, which celebrated its 75th anniversary in 1995. This is where you'll experience some of the city's best French-Creole cooking. Along with some of the old standbys, you'll find more innovative creations like pecan-stuffed salmon de la Salle in a Tabasco beurre blanc. The flaming desserts, including crepes Broussard and Bananas Foster, are superior. There's a fairly strict dress code (no jeans, shorts, sneakers, or T-shirts).

✪ Cafe Sbisa. 1011 Decatur St. ☎ **504/522-5565.** Reservations recommended. Main courses $11–$23. AE, DISC, MC, V. Sun–Thurs 5:30–10:30pm, Fri–Sat 5:30–11pm; brunch Sun 11am–3pm. NEW AMERICAN.

Located right across from the French Market, Cafe Sbisa is, after a brief closure, once again a local favorite. Cafe Sbisa first opened in 1899 and in the 1970s was one of the first to experiment with Creole cooking. There are two floors of dining rooms (tables on the upper floor near the interior balcony are the best), and there is a small courtyard. Today, Sbisa is owned by the Napoli family, which has transformed the menu so dramatically that it's nipping at the heels of Emeril's (see below) in terms of creativity. The turtle soup, I think, is the best in the city. My favorite entrée is the charcoal-grilled shrimp with a red Thai curry and barbecue relish. Desserts are equally creative; my favorite is the white chocolate bread pudding.

Court of Two Sisters. 613 Royal St. ☎ **504/522-7261.** Reservations required at dinner. Main courses $15.50–$30; fixed-price $35; brunch $21. AE, CB, DC, DISC, MC, V. Daily 9am–3pm and 5:30–10pm. CREOLE.

One of the loveliest and most atmospheric of French Quarter restaurants is the Court of Two Sisters. There are entrances from both Royal and Bourbon streets into a huge courtyard filled with flowers, fountains, and low-hanging willows, with a wishing well at its center. You can dine outside amid all that lush planting or in the Royal Court Room. An innovation here is the daily Jazz Brunch Buffet, which features more than 60 dishes and a jazz band that strolls about, supplying the New Orleans sound. Delicacies such as crawfish Louise and chicken Michelle are good bets at dinner. For dessert try the pecan pie. There is a $15 per person minimum at dinner.

Galatoire's. 209 Bourbon St. ☎ **504/525-2021.** Reservations not accepted. Jackets required after 5pm and all day Sun. Main courses $12–$24. AE, MC, V. Tues–Sat 11:30am–9pm, Sun noon–9pm. Closed holidays. FRENCH.

Galatoire's has been family run since 1905, and its traditions remain intact and unchanging. With its mirrored walls and gleaming brass fixtures, Galatoire's is one of the loveliest dining rooms in town. Seafood dishes are quite good. Oysters Rockefeller is a nice way to begin. Trout seems to be the chef's favorite fish here, and it's served in a multitude of ways. Try the trout amandine or the trout Marguéry. There is a good selection of beef, veal, and lamb, as well. At lunch, you might opt for the oysters en brochette. The à la carte menu is the same at lunch and dinner. Galatoire's doesn't accept reservations (even the visiting duke and duchess of Windsor had to wait in line), so unless you take a tip from the natives and go to lunch before noon or dinner before 6pm, you'll line up with everyone else.

K-Paul's Louisiana Kitchen. 416 Chartres St. ☎ **504/524-7394.** Reservations accepted for upstairs dining room only. Lunch $6.95–$14; dinner $20.95–$35. AE, MC, V. Mon–Sat 11:30am–2:30pm and 5:30–10pm. CAJUN.

This is the place that started all the hoopla about Cajun cooking when chef Paul Prudhomme spread its virtues across the entire country. This is also where you'll find the *hottest* interpretation of that cuisine. If it's on the menu (which changes daily), try the bronzed (just short of blackened and cooked with less butter) swordfish with "Crawfish Hot Fanny Sauce." Prudhomme's sweet potato pecan pie served with chantilly cream is probably your best bet for dessert.

The food aside, you'll have to decide if you really are prepared to wait in line (if you didn't reserve a table in the upstairs dining room) as much as an hour before gaining admittance to the plain, cafelike interior, where harried waitresses will serve you at wooden tables (sans tablecloths). You'll share the space with other diners unless your party numbers four or more. Prices have soared to *very* expensive heights, and service might be a little less attentive than you'd expect if it's busy.

Le Bistro. In the Hotel Maison de Ville, 733 Toulouse St. ☎ **504/528-9206.** Reservations recommended. Main courses $19.50–$23. AE, DC, MC, V. Mon–Sat 11:30am–2pm; daily 6–10:30pm. INTERNATIONAL.

Go to Le Bistro for some of the finest and most creative cooking in New Orleans. With white-clothed tables and a banquette running the length of the restaurant, the setting is both intimate and romantic—it seats only about 38. To start, try the crawfish with a spicy aïoli. Entrées might run the gamut from grilled sesame seed crusted yellow fin tuna (served with couscous) to herb-crusted rack of lamb. The menu changes seasonally and there's an extensive wine list.

✪ **Louis XVI.** In the St. Louis Hotel, 829 Toulouse St. ☎ **504/581-7000.** Reservations recommended. Main courses $16.50–$30. AE, CB, DC, MC, V. Mon–Fri 7–11am, Sat–Sun 7am–noon; dinner daily 6–10pm. FRENCH.

Louis XVI is one of New Orleans's finest restaurants. The elegant 1920s Parisian-style dining rooms look onto a lush courtyard complete with sparkling fountain. Tuxedoed waiters serve specialties like beef Wellington tableside. The menu, like the decor, is decidedly French, although in recent years it has been lightened slightly with the addition of dishes like filet de poisson grille au beurre de mangue (grilled fish of the day with a composed butter of mango, orange, and cilantro). However, you'll still find traditional cream sauces over shrimp and scallops and filet mignon with béarnaise sauce here. Desserts like chocolate hazelnut cake are simple but enticing.

Nola. 534 St. Louis St. ☎ **504/522-6652.** Reservations recommended. Main courses $16–$24. AE, DISC, DC, MC, V. Mon–Sat 11:30am–2pm; Sun–Thurs 6–10pm, Fri–Sat 6pm–midnight. NEW AMERICAN.

The brainchild of chef Emeril Lagasse (of Emeril's Restaurant), Nola is one of New Orleans's hottest new restaurants. A two-story establishment, Nola is modern and casual in atmosphere. Entrées at lunch include cedar plank trout with citrus-horseradish crust and lemon-butter sauce served with a spicy slaw and smoked mushroom. The Lafayette boudin stewed with beer, onions, cane syrup, and Creole mustard served on a sweet potato bread crouton is a great way to begin your dinner here. As a main course at dinner, the grilled free-range chicken with a brown sugar-cayenne rub, Caribbean style served with sweet potato casserole, guacamole and fried tortilla threads is excellent. The wine list is well selected.

✪ **Pelican Club.** 312 Exchange Alley. ☎ **504/523-1504.** Reservations recommended. Main courses $16.50–$21.50; fixed-price "early dinner" $19.50. AE, DC, DISC, MC, V. Daily 5:30–closing. Early dinner nightly 5:30–6pm. NEW AMERICAN.

The Pelican Club is located in a 19th-century Creole town house. The three distinctive dining rooms are decorated with art on consignment from area galleries. The overall cosmopolitan feeling here, combined with the talents of chefs Richard Hughes and Chin Ling, has drawn locals, visitors, and big-name stars alike. Signature dishes here include veal and shrimp potstickers with garlic-chili and ginger-soy sauces to start (the two very different sauces complement the dish well); clay pot seafood with shrimp, scallops, fish, mussels, clams, and vegetables in a broth flavored with chili, garlic, lime, and cilantro as a main course (all the shellfish in this dish are done to perfection and the decidedly Southwestern accents give the dish an unusual twist); and vanilla brandy crème brûlée for dessert. The Pelican Club has earned *Wine Spectator*'s "Award of Excellence" for the past five years running.

Peristyle. 1041 Dumaine St. ☎ **504/593-9535.** Reservations recommended. Main courses $18.50–$22.50. MC, V. Lunch Fri 11:30am–2:30pm; dinner Tues–Thurs 6–10pm, Fri–Sat 6–11pm. FRENCH/ITALIAN.

Peristyle, located on the edge of the French Quarter, is a charming place for dinner. Low light and dark wood accents set the scene for a wonderful meal. I enjoyed the beef carpaccio with shaved artichoke salad to start and moved on to the duck à l'orange. The salmon with a sorrel-wine sauce is also a fine main course. Desserts are simple, but fresh—try one of the tarts. The service staff here is extremely attentive, and the noise levels are low.

Rib Room. 621 St. Louis St. ☎ **504/529-7045.** Reservations recommended. Main courses $22–$48. AE, MC, V. Daily 11:30am–3pm; Sun–Thurs 6–10:30pm, Fri–Sat 6–11pm. SEAFOOD/STEAKS.

Ask almost any New Orleans native for a list of favorite restaurants and chances are that the Omni Hotel's Rib Room will be very near the top. Arched windows, high ceilings, natural brick, and lots of wood give the dining room a decidedly Old English feel. Open rotisserie ovens accent the back. As you might guess, the specialty is beef—prime rib ranks highest in most patrons' esteem, but there are also filets, sirloins, brochettes, tournedos, and steak au poivre. Veal, lamb, and duckling also appear on the menu, as does seafood.

MODERATE

Ⓢ Alberto's. 611 Frenchmen St. ☎ **504/949-5952.** Reservations not accepted. Main courses $7.75–$16. DISC, MC, V. Mon–Sat 6–11pm. ITALIAN.

Alberto's is a small Italian eatery above the Apple Bar with one of the friendliest staffs in the city. Alberto Gonzalez, owner and chef, holds sway in a setting of bare wooden tables, lots of hanging greenery, and a whimsical stuffed parrot. The food here is New Orleans with a touch of Italy—chicken Tasso with cream sauce and red snapper with crabmeat and capers cannelloni are a few of the specialties. The prices are amazingly low. Locals flock to this charming little place, so you may have a wait (not such a chore, with the 24-hour bar just downstairs). Frenchmen Street runs parallel to and one block behind Esplanade Avenue.

Dipiazza's. 337 Dauphine St. ☎ **504/525-3335.** Reservations recommended for dinner. Menu items $3.50–$22.95. Fixed-price from $35. AE, CB, DC, MC, V. Mon–Thurs 6–10:30pm, Fri–Sat 6–11pm. ITALIAN.

You won't see this place if you're not looking carefully or if you're on the wrong side of the street. The name is on the front of the awning, which doesn't project too far over the sidewalk. It's a casual, cozy eatery that fills up quickly for dinner, so expect to wait if you're just dropping by. The standard Italian menu items are traditionally prepared behind the wooden bar in the back. Daily specials usually bring an interesting twist to the menu. Grilled alligator makes for an unusual appetizer, and you'll usually find a grilled fish entrée or an excellent prime veal. For dessert, my favorite is the key lime cheesecake.

✪ **G&E Courtyard Grill.** 1113 Decatur St. ☎ **504/528-9376.** Reservations recommended. Main courses $12.50–$22. AE, CB, DC, DISC, MC, V. Fri–Sun 11:30am–2:30pm; Sun–Thurs 6–10pm, Fri–Sat 6–11pm. NEW AMERICAN.

Nearly seven years since its opening people are still raving about chef/proprietor Michael Uddo's creations, and there's frequently a line out the door. Go with an open mind and try something new and exciting. The soft-shell crab rolls with caviar, wasabi, and a low-salt soy sauce make an excellent starter. As an entrée, the rotisserie chicken in a mint, garlic, tomato, and balsamic sauce is unsurpassed. For dessert I can't think of anything better than the G&E's exceptionally light tiramisu. The front dining room, with a mural on one wall, is lovely; there's a nice bar as well. However, what really keeps diners coming back is the lovely covered courtyard. There actually is an open grill at the back of the courtyard, and on your left, as you walk into the courtyard, you'll also see some chefs at work.

✪ **Gabrielle.** 3201 Esplanade Ave. ☎ **504/948-6233.** Reservations recommended. Main courses $14.50–$24. AE, CB, DC, DISC, MC, V. Tues–Sat 5:30–10pm. Lunch is served 11:30am–2pm, Fri only Oct–May. INTERNATIONAL.

This uniquely shaped little restaurant, just outside the French Quarter, is gaining a big reputation around town. The white walls, hung with unpretentious pieces of art, and the white-clothed tables topped with fresh flowers create a casual and comfortable atmosphere.

The food here is superb (and something of a miracle, I think, considering the size of the kitchen). The mixed sausage grill with two sauces is also a nice way to start your meal—chef Sonnier (who studied under Paul Prudhomme and Frank Brigtsen) specializes in delectable homemade sausages. As a main course I enjoyed the panfried trout with shrimp and roasted pecan butter. Desserts are less sophisticated than they might be for a restaurant that rivals some of the best in the city, but I must say that I enjoyed my "Peppermint Patti" enormously. It's made of chocolate cake, peppermint ice cream, and chocolate sauce. There is a small bar, and the wine list is quite nice. Gabrielle offers an early evening special Tuesday through Thursday from 5:30 to 6:15pm. You'll get a choice of three appetizers, two entrées, and two desserts for only $15.95.

⑤ Gumbo Shop. 630 St. Peter St. ☎ **504/525-1486.** Reservations not required. Main courses $5.95–$14.95. AE, CB, DC, DISC, JCB, MC, V. Daily 11am–11pm. CREOLE.

In a building dating from 1795, the Gumbo Shop is just one block off Jackson Square. The atmosphere in both the small patio and the indoor dining room is informal. Murals of old New Orleans, ceiling fans, and a fireplace with an antique mirror hung above the mantel add a unique charm. The seafood gumbo here is a meal in itself, and if you haven't yet tried jambalaya this is the place to do so. Homemade desserts include southern pecan pie with ice cream. In addition to the regular menu, fresh fish entrées and dessert specialties are offered daily.

Maximo's Italian Grill. 1117 Decatur St. ☎ **504/586-8883.** Reservations recommended. Main courses $8.95–$26.95. AE, DISC, MC, V. Daily 6–11pm. ITALIAN.

A friend of mine recommended Maximo's as one of his favorite spots in New Orleans. The restaurant is done in black and gray with a slatted wood ceiling and ceiling fans, and there is an open kitchen at the back of the dining room. You can sit on a stool at the granite counter surrounding the open kitchen, at a table, in a booth, or even on the balcony. Most begin a meal here with the antipasto platter, on which you're likely to find lovely portobello mushrooms, prosciutto wrapped fruit, and a selection of olives. There are usually more than a dozen pasta dishes. The chef's signature item is veal T-bone cattoche (pan roasted with garlic and fresh herbs). Go for the Black Max (flourless chocolate cake) for dessert. This is a very popular spot, and rightly so, so be sure to make reservations. The wine list here is excellent.

Mike Anderson's Seafood. 215 Bourbon St. ☎ **504/524-3884.** Reservations not accepted. Main courses $9.95–$24.95; daily lunch specials under $8.95. AE, DISC, MC, V. Sun–Thurs 11:30am–10pm, Fri–Sat 11:30am–11pm. SEAFOOD.

This is an offshoot of the popular restaurant by the same name in Baton Rouge. As the name implies, seafood is the specialty here, and it comes in all varieties: fried, baked, boiled, or charbroiled. Especially good are the crawfish bisque and the crawfish étouffée. The daily lunch specials, served weekdays, are a bargain, and they change daily. On an average night you should be prepared to wait at least 15 minutes for a table. While you wait, you can go upstairs, have a cocktail, and sit down to some appetizers. It's not the place for a romantic evening—it can get pretty loud and crowded—but it's good food at extremely reasonable prices.

Mr. B's Bistro & Bar. 201 Royal St. ☎ **504/523-2078.** Reservations recommended. Main courses $15.50–$26. AE, DC, MC, V. Mon–Sat 11:30am–3pm; daily 5:30–10pm; brunch Sun 10:30am–3pm. CONTEMPORARY CREOLE.

Mr. B's is one of the most attractive restaurants in town, featuring polished oak floors, warm wood paneling, marble-topped tables, and large bay windows that look out onto Royal Street. You can drop in for appetizers and a salad, a casual glass of wine, or a full meal. Traditional New Orleans dishes, like seafood gumbo and Louisiana turtle soup, are featured on both the lunch and the dinner menus, but there are also some more contemporary, adventurous dishes offered, such as the skillet seared tuna with spicy ginger, red cabbage, warm mozzarella, and an herb–black pepper sauce. Recent items on the dessert menu included tangerine meringue pie and carrot cake. There's a jazz brunch on Sunday.

Olde N'Awlins Cookery. 729 Conti St. ☎ **504/529-3663.** Reservations accepted for 5 or more. Breakfast $5.75–$12.50; main courses $5.75–$14.95 at lunch, $13.50–$20.75 at dinner. AE, MC, V. Daily 8am–11pm. CREOLE/ CAJUN/SEAFOOD.

This family-operated restaurant has dished up traditional Cajun and Creole favorites and attracted a loyal local clientele. Using the freshest of Louisiana seafood and local seasonings, the kitchen turns out specialties such as Cajun jambalaya, blackened redfish, and shrimp Creole, as well as soups, salads, and great desserts. In a rather plain setting that makes use of the original old brick and a delightful courtyard, informality is the keynote.

Palm Court Café. 1204 Decatur St. ☎ **504/525-0200.** Reservations recommended. Main courses $11–$14.95. AE, DISC, MC, V. Wed–Sun 7–11pm. FRENCH/CREOLE.

The Palm Court Café is not only a delightful place to enjoy Creole and French culinary specialties but also the repository of a jazz-record collection that will probably contain any classic you might be looking for. And Wednesday through Sunday from 8 to 11pm your food comes to the table accompanied by live music from top-line jazz performers. Owners Nina and George Buck have a long history in the recording business, as well as a passionate love of food. Gumbo, shrimp Creole, oysters bordelaise, and jambalaya are just a few of the à la carte menu specials.

⑤ Port of Call. 838 Esplanade Ave. ☎ **504/523-0120.** Reservations not accepted. Main courses $6–$19. AE, MC, V. Sun–Thurs 11am–1am, Fri–Sat 11am–3am. HAMBURGERS.

After a regular diet of Cajun and Creole food, there's a point when I can't bear to look at another shrimp, oyster, or filet and can't wait to get my hands on a big, fat, juicy hamburger. That's when I head straight for Port of Call. Outside you'll see a small sign lit by a red lamp, and perhaps a line. Inside you'll find a cozy wooden interior and an attentive and friendly staff. The mushrooms sautéed in wine sauce are well known around the city, and the hamburgers, which come with a baked potato, are quite a handful. There also are pizzas, excellent filet mignon, rib eye, and New York strip steaks. Because businesspeople come from all over the city to eat here, it's often jammed at regular eating hours, so try it at off hours or before 7pm, when people who work in the Quarter gather here to relax. Port of Call also has a take-out service.

Ralph & Kacoo's. 519 Toulouse St. ☎ **504/522-5226.** Reservations not required. Main courses $6.95–$17.95. AE, DISC, MC, V. Mon–Thurs 11am–10:30pm, Fri–Sat 11am–11pm, Sun 11am–9:30pm. CREOLE/SEAFOOD.

You can't miss Ralph and Kacoo's large, colorful exterior as you walk down Toulouse, and the restaurant may well be crowded no matter when you go. But you can spend your short wait at the bar, surrounded by a lively crowd. Creole dishes, mostly seafood, are quite good and fresh, portions are more than ample, and prices are reasonable. If you're adventurous, start with the blackened alligator with hollandaise. For a main course you might try the trout Ruby, which is trout stuffed with lump crabmeat and topped with baby shrimp and hollandaise sauce. A special "heart-healthy" menu is available.

Rémoulade. 309 Bourbon St. ☎ **504/523-0377.** Reservations recommended. Full meal $15–$20. AE, CB, MC, V. Daily 11:30am–midnight. CREOLE/AMERICAN.

If you've been wanting to go to Arnaud's but can't afford it, can't get a reservation, or just don't feel like dressing up, I have the answer. It's Rémoulade, an offshoot of the famous Arnaud's (located next door). The brasserie atmosphere, with piped-in jazz music and a kitchen that can be seen from every table in the house, is a pleasant and almost downright disrespectful alternative to the traditional atmosphere of Arnaud's. The menu is fun and eclectic; the food, not surprisingly, is excellent. Thin-crust pizzas with a wide variety of toppings are popular here, as are the seafood po-boys. Rémoulade also features some of the dishes Arnaud's made famous, like shrimp Arnaud (shrimp in a Creole mustard sauce) and oysters stewed in cream. It also pokes a bit of fun at tradition by serving a hot dog topped with rémoulade sauce (it's not bad, actually). The wine list comes from Arnaud's, so you won't be disappointed on that front either.

Ristorante Carmelo. 541 Decatur St. ☎ **504/586-1414.** Reservations not required. Main courses $5.50–$9.50 at lunch, $9–$28 at dinner. AE, MC, V. Daily 11:30am–3pm; Sun–Thurs 5–11pm, Fri–Sat 5:30–11pm. ITALIAN.

Conveniently located near Jackson Brewery and Jackson Square, Ristorante Carmelo is a lovely spot for a relaxing lunch in the middle of a busy day of sightseeing, and the upstairs balcony offers a panoramic view of the Mississippi. The menu proclaims "At Carmelo you eat and drink Italian," and traditional Italian cuisine is exactly what you get. At dinner, a selection of fresh homemade pasta is available. Fresh grilled grouper, swordfish, veal dishes, carpaccio, and calamari are among the house specialties as well. For dessert, the il Nostro Tiramisu is a must.

Rita's Olde French Quarter Restaurant. 945 Chartres St. (at the corner of St. Philip). ☎ **504/525-7543.** Reservations not required. Main courses $5.95–$16.95. AE, CB, DC, DISC, MC, V. Daily 11am–10pm. CREOLE.

Rita's doesn't look like much on the outside, and you're likely to walk right by without even noticing it. Don't. When you walk in you'll feel right at home; you're likely to see members of Rita's family having dinner at the back table. There's nothing fancy here and the atmosphere is very casual. The special blackened catfish bathed in a very tasty Lea and Perrins and lemon sauce is wonderful; it's served with sweet potatoes in a brown-sugar sauce. You shouldn't miss Rita's bread pudding—and you probably won't because they often bring out a complimentary dish when you're done with your meal.

Royal Café. 700 Royal St. ☎ **504/528-9086.** Reservations not required. Main courses $4.75–$19.95. AE, MC, V. Mon–Fri 11:30am–3pm, Sat–Sun 10am–3pm; daily 5:30–10pm. CREOLE.

The balcony here finds its way into almost every tourist's photos of New Orleans. The Royal Café is a casual eatery, with dining rooms on both the ground and the second floors. But it is the upstairs balcony that appeals to most who come here. Try the "French Quarter toast" for breakfast on Saturday or Sunday. If you come later in the day, try a po-boy at lunch or the famous crabcakes at dinner. There's a terrific "Taste of New Orleans" sampler that gives you a cup of gumbo; a small bowl of red beans, sausage, and rice; followed by shrimp Creole—served with fresh-baked French bread.

Tujague's. 823 Decatur St. ☎ **504/525-8676.** Reservations recommended. Five-course lunch $6.50–$12; six-course dinner $24–$26. AE, CB, DC, DISC, MC, V. Daily 11am–3pm and 5–11pm. CREOLE.

Tujague's (pronounced *two jacks*) is the second restaurant to occupy this site. The first was run by Madame Begue, who in 1856 began cooking huge "second breakfasts" for the butchers who worked in the French Market across the way. Today Tujague's serves only lunch and dinner, but continues the original cook's tradition of serving whatever inspiration dictates that day. This is a favorite with New Orleanians, who seem not to mind that there's a very limited menu. At lunch, you have a choice of three entrées, which might include the freshest fish available that day. The five-course meal will consist of soup, salad, entrée, vegetable, dessert, and beverage. If something lighter appeals to you, choose gumbo served with a side dish of shrimp salad.

INEXPENSIVE

"Inexpensive" in the French Quarter can often mean "very, very good." That's due, I think, to two things: First, many traditional dishes here are made with low-cost ingredients (red beans and rice, for example); second, there are so many good cooks in this city who can make almost anything taste delicious. So toss aside your preconceived notions about luncheonette-style eateries, and try one or two of the following.

⑤ Acme Oyster House. 724 Iberville St. ☎ **504/522-5973.** Reservations not accepted. Oysters $3.50–$6; New Orleans specialties $5.25–$5.75; seafood $7.75–$9.75; po-boys $4–$5. AE, DC, JCB, MC, V. Mon–Sat 11am–10pm, Sun noon–7pm. SEAFOOD.

If you're an oyster lover, there's nothing quite like standing at the oyster bar in the Acme Oyster House, eating a dozen or so freshly shucked oysters on the half shell. (You can have them at a table, but somehow they taste better at the bar.) If you can't quite stomach them raw, try the oyster po-boy off the sandwich menu, with beer, of course, as the perfect accompaniment. Acme offers fresh baked bread pudding and cheesecake on the dessert menu.

Café Maspero. 601 Decatur St. ☎ **504/523-6250.** Reservations not accepted. Main courses $4–$8.50. No credit cards. Sun–Thurs 11am–11pm, Fri–Sat 11am–midnight. SEAFOOD/SANDWICHES.

The Café Maspero serves the largest portions I've run into—burgers, deli sandwiches, seafood, and so on—as well as an impressive list of wines, beers, and cocktails, all at low, low prices. This is a lively and popular spot, especially with the after-theater crowd; it's not unusual to see a line. But it's worth your time to wait—the quality is as good as the portions are large.

Felix's Restaurant & Oyster Bar. 739 Iberville St. ☎ **504/522-4440.** Reservations not required. Main courses $10–$16.95. AE, MC, V. Mon–Thurs 10:30am–midnight, Fri–Sat 10:30am–1:30am, Sun 10:30am–10pm. SEAFOOD/CREOLE.

If you get a yen for oysters, go to Felix's. Like its neighbor, the Acme Oyster House, Felix's is almost legendary among New Orleanians, and it stays open quite late all week long. Sometimes crowded and noisy, it almost always looks disorganized, but if you pass it by on those grounds you'll be missing a memorable experience. Have your oysters raw, in a stew, in a soup, Rockefeller or Bienville style, in your spaghetti, or even in your omelet. In addition to the oysters, there's a selection of fried or grilled fish, chicken, and steaks, and the Creole cooking is quite good. It's possible to get things blackened to order.

Louisiana Pizza Kitchen. 2800 Esplanade Ave. ☎ **504/488-2800.** Reservations not required. Pizzas $5.95–$7.95, pastas $4.50–$9.95. AE, CB, DC, DISC, MC, V. Daily 5:30–11pm. ITALIAN.

The Louisiana Pizza Kitchen is favored locally for its creative pies as well as for the atmosphere. Located on a quiet section of Esplanade Avenue, its dining room allows patrons a lovely view. While pastas also have a place on the menu, it's the pizza and Caesar salad that diners come for. Individually sized pizzas, baked in a wood-fired oven, are offered with a wide variety of toppings (shrimp pizza and roasted garlic pizza are two of the most popular). And your toppings won't get lost in an abundance of cheese and tomato sauce.

Louisiana Pizza Kitchen is also located at 95 French Market Place (☎ **504/522-9500**) and 615 S. Carrollton Ave. (☎ **504/866-5900**).

Mama Rosa's. 616 N. Rampart St. ☎ **504/523-5546.** Reservations not required. Pizzas $7.25–$13.50; specials $5–$7.50. MC, V. Tues–Thurs, Sun 10:30am–10:30pm; Fri–Sat 10:30am–11:30pm. ITALIAN.

Mama Rosa's "Little Slice of Italy" serves up a big slice of pizza. While the decor is nothing to brag about—typical red and white checkered linen tablecloths, a jukebox, and a bar—the pizzas are. You can get a 10- or 14-inch pizza with a variety of different toppings for very reasonable prices. The crusts are thick, and the more you put on them, the better they are. In fact, the slices are so thick, you could almost compare them to pan pizza. Of course, you can also get pasta and the salads are big enough to be a full meal. You can even get mini muffalettas as appetizers. One of the big draws is Mama Rosa's homemade bread. The staff can be a bit surly, but most people don't go there for ambience; they go with one thing in mind: good, fast, inexpensive Italian food. And they get it.

Napoleon House. 500 Chartres St. (at the corner of St. Louis). ☎ **504/524-9752.** Reservations required for large parties. Sandwiches and pastries $4.25–$10. AE, MC, V. Daily 11am–1am. AMERICAN/ITALIAN.

Giving in a bit to everyday wear and tear on the outside, Napoleon House is so named because at the time of the death of the "Little Corporal" there was actually a plot (most likely absinthe induced) hatching in this 1797 National Landmark to snatch him from his island exile and bring him to New Orleans. The third floor was added expressly for the purpose of providing him with a home after the rescue. It wears its history with dignity. There's a limited menu of po-boys, Italian muffuletta sandwiches, and pastries; the jukebox plays only classical music. You can relax inside by the old bar or outside in the courtyard. This is a very popular spot with visiting celebrities and locals who gather after dark.

New Orleans Coffee & Concierge. 334B Royal St. ☎ **504/524-5530.** Reservations not necessary. All items $1.67–$6.95. MC, V (in gallery only). Daily 8am–5pm. CAFE.

When I first discovered New Orleans Coffee and Concierge in 1992 it was a new addition to the French Quarter scene. Four years later it's more popular than ever. It has been transformed from a small cafe serving pastries and coffee into a full-service, bistro-style cafe offering breakfast and lunch, and there is a gallery that at press time was featuring the works of George Rodrique, world famous for his "Blue Dog" paintings. At breakfast you can get Belgian waffles, an omelet soufflé, bagels and lox, and brioche French toast. Items on the lunch menu include gumbo, crawfish pie, vegetable sandwiches, and salads. They're now serving the famous New Orleans beignets, and there's an exclusive Robert Mondavi Wine Bar available for tastings all afternoon.

Père Antoine Restaurant. 714 Royal St. ☎ **504/581-4478.** Reservations not required. Main courses $3.95–$14.95. No credit cards. Daily 9am–midnight. CAJUN/CREOLE.

Père Antoine is an attractive European-style place with huge mirrors in back and flowers out front. Specialties here include Cajun red snapper (cooked in a rich tomato sauce, a nice change from "blackened"), shrimp, and crawfish étouffée. For lighter meals, there are soups and salads, sandwiches and burgers, omelets, and such New Orleans favorites as red beans and rice, jambalaya, and chicken Creole. Items on the breakfast menu, such as Belgian waffles and a "Louisiana Breakfast—The Rajun Cajun Omelet" (with smoked sausage, green peppers, onion, ham, and a Creole sauce), are available all day.

Petunia's. 817 St. Louis St. ☎ **504/522-6440.** Reservations not required. Main courses $9.95–$18.95. AE, DISC, MC, V. Daily 8am–11pm. CAJUN/CREOLE.

Petunia's, located in an 1830s town house between Bourbon and Dauphine streets, dishes up enormous portions of New Orleans specialties like shrimp Creole, Cajun pasta with shrimp and andouille, and a variety of fresh seafoods. Breakfast and Sunday brunch are popular here, with a broad selection of crepes—they are billed as the world's largest (I can't prove it, but they probably are) at 14 inches. Crepe selections include the "St. Francis," filled with shrimp, crab ratatouille, and Swiss cheese. If you have room for dessert, try the dessert crepes or the peanut butter pie.

✪ **Praline Connection.** 542 Frenchmen St. ☎ **504/943-3934.** Reservations not accepted. Main courses $4–$13.95. AE, DC, DISC, MC, V. Sun–Thurs 11am–10:30pm, Fri–Sat 11am–midnight. CREOLE/SOUL FOOD.

The Praline Connection is famous around the city, but visitors probably wouldn't know about it unless it was recommended to them by a friend—it's hidden away on Frenchmen Street, which is just behind Esplanade Avenue. The interior is bright and airy, with stainless-steel ceiling fans and a black and white tiled floor. It's not where you'd go for a romantic dinner (the noise level can be quite daunting). People go to eat and have fun; you might end up talking to the people next to you because sometimes there is not enough room to seat you at a private table. The food is wonderful, plentiful, and very reasonably priced—it's real southern soul cooking at its best. The fried chicken is crispy and juicy. There are red beans, white beans, and crowder peas, as well as okra, mustard greens, and collard greens.

A small candy shop is attached (there are a few tables in there, and it's a little quieter than the main dining room) selling pralines as well as other candies. Praline Connection II at 901 South Peters St. (☎ 504/523-3973) offers the same menu and a larger dining room.

St. Ann's Cafe & Deli. 800 Dauphine St. (at the corner of St. Ann). ☎ **504/ 529-4421.** $2.25–$12.95. AE, DISC, MC, V. Open 24 hrs. CAFE/DELI.

St. Ann's is a cozy little cafe. There's nothing fancy about it—it's more of a local hangout than a tourist attraction. Everything here is homemade, and you can get a variety of foods, including sandwiches, pizzas, soups, and salads, as well as breakfast items. Lunch and dinner specials are offered daily, and there's a decent selection of beer and wine.

4 Downtown

Christian's. 3835 Iberville St. ☎ **504/482-4924.** Reservations recommended. Main courses $13.25–$23.95. AE, CB, DC, MC, V. Tues–Fri 11:30am–2pm and 5:30–10pm; Sat 5:30–10pm. FRENCH/CREOLE.

Ever had a three-course meal in a church? Christian Ansel renovated the interior of this little church to house his restaurant, but the exterior remains unaltered. Seafood dished are the specialty here, some of which are prepared with the most delicate of French sauces. Try the crawfish "Carolyn" (crawfish in a spicy cream sauce with brandy and Parmesan cheese) to start; the shrimp en brochette (grilled shrimp with slices of onion and bell pepper served with a lemon butter sauce over angel hair pasta) as an entrée; and finish it off with baked Alaska or profiteroles aux chocolate. There are specials available at lunch.

Dooky Chase. 2301 Orleans Ave. ☎ **504/821-2294.** Reservations recommended at dinner. Fixed-price $26; main courses $10.50–$19.50; Creole feast $39.50. AE, DC, MC, V. Daily 11:30am–midnight. SOUL FOOD/CREOLE.

Established in 1941, Dooky Chase has long been a favorite of the locals, but it's only just recently been recognized by critics farther afield as serving some of the best soul food in the city. And Leah Chase is fast becoming known as one of the great chefs of New

Orleans. Chase dishes up soul food with distinctive New Orleans touches, such as shrimp Dooky with its spicy rémoulade sauce. And the fried chicken here is terrific, some of the best I've had in a long time. Try the praline pudding for dessert. If you're really in the mood to put on a few pounds, call and reserve a Creole feast for yourself. *Note:* After dark, it is best to go there by cab.

✪ **Ruth's Chris Steak House.** 711 N. Broad St. ☎ **504/486-0810.** Reservations recommended. Main courses $8.50–$28.50. AE, DC, MC, V. Daily 11:30am–11pm. STEAKS.

You won't get an argument locally if you pronounce that the best steak in town is served at Ruth's Chris Steak House. The specialty here is, in fact, prime beef, custom aged, cut by hand, and beautifully prepared. All the beef prepared at Ruth's Chris Steak House is corn fed. Pork chops and one or two other meats appear on the menu, but this is primarily a steak house, and one that will not disappoint.

There's another Ruth's Chris at 3633 Veterans Blvd. in Metairie (☎ **504/888-3600**).

5 Central Business District

EXPENSIVE

✪ **Emeril's.** 800 Tchoupitoulas St. ☎ **504/528-9393.** Reservations recommended at dinner. Main courses $7.50–$25. AE, CB, DC, DISC, MC, V. Mon–Fri 11:30am–2pm and 6–10pm; Sat 6–10pm. CREOLE/NEW AMERICAN.

Emeril Lagasse, who used to be head chef at Commander's Palace, is another of the young, daring, but traditionally schooled chefs that has been causing a stir in New Orleans. He has gained national recognition with his own show, "The Essence of Emeril," on the Food Network.

The restaurant is the warehouse district, practically on gallery row. The building was, in fact, once a warehouse, and rather than cover the remaining traces of its history, Lagasse has incorporated exposed pipes in the interior design and created a wonderfully modern establishment.

Lagasse insists on making everything from scratch—even the ketchup. Emeril loves experimenting with new ingredients and preparations while still improving on the old stand-bys. To start, try the grilled homemade andouille sausage with his famous homemade Worcestershire sauce. As an entrée you might have the panéed Mississippi quail (sautéed in olive oil until crisp and served with roasted garlic, smashed root vegetables, crispy bacon, green beans, stewed barbecue quail legs, and a drizzle of sweet barbecue sauce). The incredible desserts include banana cream pie with a banana-flavored crust and topped with caramel sauce and chocolate shavings. Emeril now employs a full-time sommelier and the wine list recently won recognition and awards from *Wine Spectator* magazine.

✪ **Graham's.** 200 Magazine St. ☎ **504/524-9678.** Reservations recommended, especially on weekends. Main courses $14–$24 at dinner. AE, CB, DC, DISC, MC, V. Breakfast daily 7–10:30am; lunch Mon–Fri 11:30am–2pm; dinner Sun–Thurs 6–10pm, Fri–Sat 6–11pm. ECLECTIC.

Graham's is one of New Orleans's most recently opened restaurants. From 1988 to 1994 Kevin Graham was the head chef at the Grill Room in the Windsor Court Hotel. Now he works his magic at his own place. The modern dining room here has soaring ceilings, tile floors, and few decorative accents. Menus change very frequently, but if you get a chance, you should try the foie gras served with cubes of port-wine aspic and sauced with red currant jelly, ginger, mustard, and shallots. The veal chop I had, which was served with tomato sauce and accompanied by a white bean and fontina puree, was excellent. Desserts like the lemon tart are simple, but well-executed. The wine list is excellent.

✪ **The Veranda Restaurant.** In the Hotel Inter-Continental, 444 St. Charles Ave. ☎ **504/525-5566.** Reservations recommended. Main courses $11.50–$22.50. AE, CB, DC, DISC, MC, V. Mon–Sat 11am–2pm and 5:30–10pm, Sun 5:30–9pm; brunch Sun 11am–2:30pm. CONTINENTAL/CREOLE.

The atmosphere at The Veranda is both dramatic and comfortable—its glass-enclosed garden courtyard and private dining room make you feel as though you're dining in a stately New Orleans home. And The Veranda's chef, Willy Coln, is one of the most respected in New Orleans. The menu is varied, and it is doubtful that you'll find anything to complain about. Appetizers include smoked duck and wild mushroom strudel. For an entrée I enjoyed potato crusted redfish with baby bok choy and a ginger beurre blanc. Desserts are incredible, and I know because I tasted every one.

MODERATE

Bailey's. In the Fairmont Hotel, 123 University Place (entrance at Baronne St). ☎ **504/529-7111.** Reservations not required. All items $3–$17. AE, CB, DC, DISC, MC, V. Sun–Thurs 11am–1am, Fri–Sat 24 hours. COFFEE SHOP.

Bailey's is a cozy spot softly lit by Tiffany-style lamps and decorated with antiques. At any hour of the day you can order breakfast, or New Orleans specialties such as red beans and rice with hot sausage.

There also are sandwiches and burgers, as well as a nice selection of po-boys.

Bon Ton Café. 401 Magazine St. ☎ **504/524-3386.** Reservations required at dinner. Main courses $8.75–$14.50 at lunch, $18.75–$24.25 at dinner. AE, DC, MC, V. Mon–Fri 11am–2pm and 5–9:30pm. CAJUN.

You'll find the Bon Ton Café absolutely mobbed at lunch with businesspeople and their guests. Such popularity is largely due to its owner, Al Pierce; his nephew, Wayne; and Wayne's wife, Debbie. Al and Wayne both grew up in the Bayou country, where Al learned Cajun cooking from his mother. He came to New Orleans in 1936, bought the Bon Ton in 1953, and since then has been serving up Cajun dishes in a manner that would make his mother proud. Wayne and Debbie are continuing the tradition. This is a small, utterly charming place that's not to be missed if you want to sample true Cajun cooking at its best.

Kabby's Seafood Restaurant. 2 Poydras St. ☎ **504/584-3880.** Reservations recommended. Main courses $17–$28.95. AE, CB, DC, MC, V. Daily 10:30am–2:30pm and 6–11pm. SEAFOOD.

Dining at Kabby's affords a spectacular lookout over the river through a 200-foot-wide, 14-foot-high window. You enter the restaurant through a New Orleans courtyard foyer. At lunch, there are salads, sandwiches (oyster loaf, muffuletta, and so on), and other specialties. The dinner menu is more adventurous. To start, try the crabmeat stuffed oysters with a trio of dipping sauces. As a main course, the peppered duck breast (with andouille sausage dressing, sweet potato frites, and a natural duck reduction) is excellent. The warm pecan and chocolate tart is a good choice for dessert.

✪ **Palace Café.** 605 Canal St. ☎ **504/523-1661.** Reservations recommended. Main courses $9.95–$20. AE, CB, MC, V. Lunch Mon–Sat 11:30am–2:30pm; brunch Sun 10:30am–2:30pm, dinner daily 5:30–7:30pm. CONTEMPORARY CREOLE.

Operated by Ti Martin, daughter of Ella Brennan, the Palace Café is a grand cafe serving contemporary Creole seafood. Enter through the brass and glass revolving door and you will be immediately impressed by the spiral staircase in the middle of the restaurant. It's comfortable, the ground floor being almost entirely made up of booths—even for two. Upstairs you'll find a mural featuring local music giants, such as Aaron Neville, Harry Connick Jr., Ellis Marsalis, and Louis Armstrong.

No doubt you'll find something interesting on the menu. If you're an oyster lover, start with the oyster shooters (raw oysters served in a shot glass). The seafood boil features the day's fresh local seafood served on a raised platter (just the way it's done in the grand cafes of Paris). The crabmeat cheesecake is excellent, as is the grilled tuna. Perfect rotisserie roasted pork chops and chicken are also available. For dessert, you should try the white chocolate bread pudding. If you go for lunch there's likely to be a large business crowd present. Brunch on Sunday brings live blues by Betty Shirley.

INEXPENSIVE

Bluebird Cafe. 3625 Prytania St. ☎ **504/895-7166.** Reservations not accepted. All menu items under $7. No credit cards. Mon–Fri 8am–3pm, Sat–Sun 7am–3pm. AMERICAN.

The charming eggshell blue dining room at the Bluebird Cafe is always packed, primarily with a local crowd of breakfast and lunch diners in the know. This place is one of the best in New Orleans to stop for a hearty, flavorful, inexpensive meal. Portions are enormous. Try the buckwheat pecan waffle or the cheese grits (my favorite); they even make their own sausage.

Ernst's Café. 600 S. Peters St. ☎ **504/525-8544.** Reservations not required. Main courses $6.50–$9.95. AE, DC, MC, V. Mon–Sat 11am–3pm. CAJUN/CREOLE.

There's been an eatery and bar run by the same family in the old brick building that now houses Ernst's Café since 1902. Its brick walls, high ceilings, and heavy timbered bar make it an interesting and attractive setting for excellent sandwiches, hamburgers, fried shrimp, salads, red beans and rice, and po-boys. If the weather is fine, eat outside.

⑤ Mother's. 401 Poydras St. ☎ **504/523-9656.** Reservations not accepted. Menu items $1.75–$16.50. No credit cards. Mon–Sat 5am–10pm, Sun 7am–10pm. SANDWICHES/CREOLE.

You owe it to yourself to make at least one pilgrimage to Mother's. Be sure to allow time to stand in line—bankers line up with warehouse workers, dockworkers, and just about everybody else from this part of town for *the* best po-boy sandwiches in New Orleans. Made on crisp French bread fresh from the oven, the po-boys here are real creations. Many of them are served with a rich, thick, sloppy gravy, but the sandwiches are so good you won't mind the mess. The restaurant's most sought-after po-boy is the Ferdi Special with baked ham, roast beef, shredded cabbage, and Creole mustard. There are plate lunches, too, such as the excellent gumbo, red beans, Jerry's award-winning jambalaya, and spaghetti pie, and they also serve one of the best breakfasts in the city. Mother's is always crowded, but don't let that throw you off—the line moves quickly.

Uglesich's Restaurant & Bar. 1238 Barrone St. ☎ **504/523-8571.** Reservations not required. Lunch $6–$11. No credit cards. Mon–Fri 9:30am–4pm. SANDWICHES.

Uglesich's, at Erato Street near Lee Circle, is old and more than a little rundown in appearance (stacked cases of beer are some of the most decorative features this place has to offer), but it is well loved locally for its outstanding sandwiches of fried food. Leave your jacket behind or you'll carry the fried smell all day.

6 Uptown (Including the Garden District)

EXPENSIVE

Brigtsen's. 723 Dante St. ☎ **504/861-7610.** Reservations required a week or two in advance. Main courses $12–$24. AE, DC, MC, V. Tues–Sat 5:30–10pm. CAJUN/CREOLE.

In the Riverbend area, Brigtsen's occupies a small house and is presided over by Frank Brigtsen, a former chef at K-Paul's. The menu changes daily, but recent dishes included roast duck with "dirty" rice and honey-pecan gravy, and broiled Gulf fish with a crabmeat Parmesan crust and lemon mousselline. For those on a budget, Brigtsen's offers "Early Evening" dinner specials Tuesday through Thursday from 5:30 to 6:30pm. The price, $14.95, includes a three-course dinner.

Caribbean Room. In the Pontchartrain Hotel, 2031 St. Charles Ave. ☎ **504/524-0581.** Reservations recommended. Main courses $19–$31.50. AE, DC, DISC, MC, V. Tues–Sat 6–10pm. FRENCH/CREOLE.

Since it opened in 1948, the Caribbean Room has won a list of culinary awards as long as your arm, and it really epitomizes New Orleans cuisine at its finest. The decor, like that of the rest of the hotel, is infused with a refined (almost understated) luxury. The kitchen turns out appetizer specialties such as crabmeat Remick served with tortilla chips. Brilliantly executed main courses like duckling vert pres (slow-roasted half duckling on mixed greens with orange-fig gravy and poached pear) are the things that keep diners coming back, and the Mile-High Pie is what makes them stay for dessert.

✪ **Commander's Palace.** 1403 Washington Ave. (at the corner of Coliseum St.). ☎ **504/899-8221.** Reservations required, sometimes days in advance. Main courses $22–$30; full brunch $20–$32; full dinner $29–$32. AE, CB, DC,

MC, V. Mon–Fri 11:30am–2pm; daily 6–10pm; brunch Sat 11:30am–12:30pm
and Sun 10:30am–1pm. HAUTE CREOLE.

The unusual, rather grand blue-and-white Victorian building was
built as a restaurant in 1880 by Emile Commander and is now
owned by members of the Brennan family. Commander's Palace is
a consistent favorite of locals and visitors alike. The patio, fountains,
lush tropical plantings, and soft colors are a perfect backdrop for
mouthwatering Creole specialties. To start your meal try the Soups
1-1-1, a half serving of turtle soup au sherry, Creole gumbo du jour,
and the soup of the day. Outstanding entrées include roasted Mississippi quail with a rock shrimp stuffing and a port-wine sauce.
Commander's also has a nice roast rack of lamb for two with a mint-
Madeira demi-glacé. There is an excellent wine list, and the menu
offers suggestions with each entrée. If you're a jazz buff, don't miss
their famous Jazz Brunch, featuring Joe Simon and his Dixieland
band.

✪ **Mike's on the Avenue.** In the Lafayette Hotel, 628 St. Charles Ave.
☎ **504/523-1709.** Reservations recommended. Main courses at lunch $11–
$15, at dinner $18–$26. AE, MC, V. Mon–Fri 11:30am–2pm; daily 6–10pm.
NEW AMERICAN.

Mike's on the Avenue has become a local hot spot over the past
few years. Chef Mike Fennelly is inspired not only in the creation
of dishes—like his homemade Chinese dumplings filled with
shrimp, ginger, and scallions with a Szechuan tahini sauce—but
also in the creation of the canvases that decorate the walls of his
restaurant. The eclectic cuisine crosses the borders of many countries—traditional Louisiana crabcakes are emboldened with the spice
of chiles and smoothed by a lobster cream. Desserts are equally
creative. My favorite is the brioche bread pudding. This is not
the place for a quiet, romantic dinner for two: It's a lively spot
and the high ceilings and the prevalence of glass don't absorb the
noise.

Pascal's Manale. 1838 Napoleon Ave. ☎ **504/895-4877.** Reservations recommended. Main courses $13.95–$22. AE, DC, DISC, MC, V. Mon–Fri
11:30am–10pm, Sat 4–10pm, Sun 4–9pm. Closed Sun Memorial Day through
Labor Day. ITALIAN/STEAKS/SEAFOOD.

Locals still flock to Pascal's Manale for barbecued shrimp. It's
crowded, noisy, and verges on expensive, but you'll leave as much
a fan as any native. Don't expect fancy decor—the emphasis is on
food and conviviality. (Sunday nights feel more like social gatherings than one could reasonably expect at a commercial restaurant.)

✪ **Sazerac.** In the Fairmont Hotel, 123 Baronne St. ☎ **504/529-4733.** Reservations recommended. Jackets recommended at dinner. Main courses $14.95–$24.95. Fixed-price $21. AE, CB, DC, DISC, MC, V. Mon–Fri 11:30am–2pm; daily 6–10pm. CREOLE/CONTINENTAL.

The dining room features cut-glass chandeliers, lace-covered tables, and red velvet banquettes. A meal here begins with such appetizers as steak tartare (prepared tableside). Main courses include Louisiana Gulf shrimp (stuffed with lump crabmeat and fresh herbs) and steak Diane. For dessert go for the sorbet served in illuminated ice swans. Brunch on Sunday features three special menus. The wine list is excellent.

Upperline. 1413 Upperline (between St. Charles Ave. and Prytania St.). ☎ **504/891-9822.** Reservations required. Main courses $8.95–$17.50. AE, DC, MC, V. Mon, Wed–Sun 5:30–9:30pm. ECLECTIC/CREOLE.

Upperline is a small, popular uptown place whose walls are decorated with the colorful works of local artists. Chef Richard Benz continues a rich 14-year heritage of a varied, creative, Creole-inspired menu, keeping many old favorites and adding new ones of his own. The restaurant's most popular dishes of late include onion crusted redfish and rack of lamb in a spicy Merlot sauce. If you can't decide, give the seven course "Taste of New Orleans" dinner a try. For dessert try the warm honey-pecan bread pudding or the chocolate hazelnut mousse. An award-winning wine list focuses primarily on California selections.

The Versailles. 2100 St. Charles Ave. ☎ **504/524-2535.** Reservations recommended. Main courses $20–$29. AE, MC, V. Mon–Sat 6–10pm. FRENCH/CREOLE.

For dining in high style, you just can't equal The Versailles. Chef Dennis Hutley creates specialties such as smoked venison with a pinot noir aspic and pan-roasted snapper in an almond crust (served on sautéed crabmeat with a poblano pepper cream sauce). Baking is done on the premises (try the hazelnut cake Marjolaine) and the wine cellar is outstanding. Valet parking is free.

MODERATE

Casamento's. 4330 Magazine St. ☎ **504/895-9761.** Reservations not accepted. Main courses $2.40–$9.40. No credit cards. Tues–Sun 11:30am–1:30pm and 5:30–9pm. Closed mid-June to mid-Sept. SEAFOOD.

The plain exterior fronts a warm, friendly restaurant decorated with Spanish tiles and lots of plants. Almost always crowded (mostly with locals), Casamento's has an excellent oyster bar and some of the best seafood plates in town at unbelievably low prices. Their oyster loaf is especially good. But don't confuse the oyster loaf with the oyster sandwich—the loaf is made with a large loaf of white bread toasted and buttered and filled with fried oysters and large enough for two; the sandwich comes on regular toast. The same goes for the shrimp loaf and the tenderloined trout loaf.

✪ **Copeland's.** 4339 St. Charles Ave. ☎ **504/897-2325.** Reservations recommended. Main courses $8–$15.95. AE, CB, DC, DISC, MC, V. Mon–Fri 11:30am–1:30pm; daily 6–10pm; brunch Sat 11:30am–12:30pm, Sun 10am–12:30pm. CAJUN/CREOLE.

Copeland's, uptown, almost operates on a fast-food basis, yet its dishes are so authentic and fresh that it has gained a loyal local following. The setting is attractive with dark wood, brass, and glass accents; all the ingredients are fresh; and the recipes have been collected from some of New Orleans's leading chefs. Copeland's current chef, George Rhode IV, worked in the kitchens of K-Paul's, Olde N'Awlins Cookery, and his own restaurant, George IV. Start with the onion mumm, a local favorite. One of my top choices for dinner is the grilled chicken with spinach and bacon dressing topped with blue cheese. For dessert, the sweet potato and pecan bread pudding is a delicious twist on the traditional version.

Delmonico Restaurant. 1300 St. Charles Ave. ☎ **504/525-4937.** Reservations not required. Main courses $16–$23. AE, DC, DISC, MC, V. Daily 11:30am–9pm. SEAFOOD/STEAKS.

A short streetcar ride from the Quarter, the Delmonico Restaurant was founded in 1895 and has been run by the La Franca family since 1911; many of the dishes on the menu actually come from old family recipes. Delmonico is essentially a comfortable, family-style eatery, with a touch of elegance. As a dedicated seafood lover, I favor the Delmonico seafood kebab (shrimp, oysters, trout, and red snapper), but the steaks, veal, and chicken dishes are also very good. Desserts are simple but acceptable.

Gautreau's. 1728 Soniat St. ☎ **504/899-7397.** Reservations recommended. Main courses $12.50–$21. AE, MC, V. Tues–Sat 6–10pm. INTERNATIONAL.

Those of you who knew the old Gautreau's (which, after closing in 1989 was reopened by new owners) won't be disappointed to see that the new Gautreau's warm and modest decor has remained the same: the tin ceiling, the old New Orleans photographs, and the famous apothecary cabinet from the original drugstore that still holds a varied selection of wines. Menus change seasonally, but if it's on the menu you should try the marinated shrimp and Dungeness crab served with sticky rice and an orange and honey soy sauce to start. As an entrée, the sautéed tilapia and shrimp with basmati rice, arugula, and chile mango sauce is wonderful. The pastry chef does a delightful triple layer (chocolate, maple pecan, and almond) cheesecake.

Tavern on the Park. 900 City Park Ave. ☎ **504/486-3333.** Reservations recommended. Main courses $15.95–$24.95. AE, CB, DC, JCB, MC, V. Tues– Fri 11:30am–2:30pm and 5–10pm; Sat 5–10pm or later. Closed Sun–Mon. SEAFOOD/STEAKS.

Just across from City Park, within sight of the famous "dueling oaks," the Tavern on the Park is a delightful re-creation of Art Deco eateries of the Prohibition era and is, in fact, the only remaining building from the Storyville era. The historic building is a marvelous setting for the restaurant's steak and seafood specialties, with broiled cold-water lobster, fresh trout, and superb steaks high on the list of local favorites. Balcony dining is available, weather permitting.

INEXPENSIVE

⑤ Camellia Grill. 626 S. Carrollton Ave. ☎ **504/866-9573.** All items under $10. No credit cards. Sun–Thurs 9am–1am, Fri–Sat 9am–3am. HAMBURGERS/ SANDWICHES.

If you're out in the Riverbend area, don't bypass the Camellia Grill. It's right on the trolley line and serves a great variety of sandwiches, omelets, salads, and desserts at low to moderate prices. The hamburgers are really special; the sandwiches are stuffed to overflowing; and the omelets are enormous. And although it's counter service, surprisingly, you'll be given a real linen napkin.

7 Metairie

Bozo's. 3117 21st St. ☎ **504/831-8666.** Reservations not required. Lunch $5–$10; dinner $12–$16. MC, V. Tues–Sat 11am–3pm; Tues–Thurs 5–10pm, Fri–Sat 5–11pm. CAJUN/SEAFOOD.

New Orleanians have much affection for this plain, unpretentious fish house. Almost anything that swims or lives in nearby waters makes its way onto the menu, which also includes a few steak, chicken, and veal selections; and a good list of sandwiches.

Crozier's Restaurant Français. 3216 W. Esplanade, N. Metairie. ☎ **504/ 833-8108.** Reservations recommended. Main courses $15.25–$19.50. AE, DC, DISC, MC, V. Tues–Sat 5:30–10pm. FRENCH.

Authentic French cooking accounts for this restaurant's long-standing popularity. Begin with a very tasty, traditional onion soup or a salad of mixed greens. There's also a nice duck liver pâté and of course, the ever-present escargots. If you've had enough sea-food on this trip to last you a while, chef Gerard Crozier makes a wonderful steak au poivre and an incredible grilled quail with a light demi-glacé. Traditional desserts like crème caramel and mousse au chocolate are a nice way to finish a meal here. The wine list is limited but good and moderately priced.

8 Coffee, Tea & Sweets

Angelo Brocato's Ice Cream & Confectionery. 537 St. Ann St. ☎ **504/525-9676.** All items under $8. No credit cards. Mon–Fri 10am–6pm, Sat 10am–11pm, Sun 9am–8pm. ITALIAN PASTRY.

There's been a Brocato's in New Orleans since 1905, and except for a brief interruption, it has been in the French Quarter. It is the Brocato's on whom the city's most demanding hostesses have depended for three generations to cater those occasions for friends and special guests when sweets must reach the heights of sheer perfection. Happily you'll now find them back in new quarters, serving their fabulous ice cream, Italian ices, cannolis, and a whole feast of other pastries.

There's another branch at 214 N. Carrollton Ave. (☎ **504/486-0078**).

Café du Monde. In the French Market, 813 Decatur. ☎ **504/581-2914.** Coffee, milk, hot chocolate, and beignets $1. No credit cards. Daily 24 hrs. Closed Christmas Day. CAFE.

This is one of my favorites, an indispensable part of the New Orleans food scene. Across from Jackson Square and absolutely habit-forming, the delightful Café du Monde has been a favorite with New Orleanians for years. There are only four main items on the menu—coffee (black or au lait), milk, hot chocolate, and beignets (three to a serving)—and each item costs $1. Beignets (pronounced *bin-YEAS*), the official doughnuts of Louisiana, are square, deep-fried confections that come hot, crisp, and covered with confectioner's sugar. There's an indoor dining room, but sit outside under the awning to take advantage of the Mississippi River breeze and unexcelled people-watching. You'll find many a native here in the dawn or predawn hours.

La Madeleine. 547 St. Ann St. (at Chartres St.). ☎ **504/568-9950.** Pastries 85¢–$2.25; entrées $3.89–$9.25. AE, MC, V. Daily 7am–10pm. FRENCH BAKERY.

La Madeleine is one of the French Quarter's most charming casual eateries. One of a chain of French bakeries, it has a wood-burning brick oven that turns out a wide variety of breads, croissants, and brioches. A glass case up front holds marvelous pastries to take out or eat in the cafeteria section, where quiches, salads, soups, sandwiches, and other light entrées are available.

La Marquise. 625 Chartres St. ☎ **504/524-0420.** Pastries 82¢–$5. No credit cards. Daily 7am–5pm. PASTRY.

The tiny La Marquise serves French pastries on the premises, either in a crowded front room that also holds the display counter or outside on a small but delightful patio. Pastries run the gamut from pain au chocolat (a rectangle of croissant dough that has been wrapped around a chocolate bar, then baked) to croissants, brioches, and a wide assortment of strudels and Danish pastries. La Marquise is almost always crowded; if the patio has no seats available, there's always Jackson Square just a few steps away for a dessert picnic.

A larger La Marquise is at 617 Ursulines St.

P. J.'s Coffee & Tea Company. 5432 Magazine St. ☎ **504/895-0273.** 80¢–$4. AE, MC, V. Daily 7am–11pm. COFFEE/PASTRIES.

P. J.'s is just the place if you're mad about tea or coffee—you can taste as many as 18 teas and three or four coffees on any given day. Their newest addition is granita prepared with P. J.'s own Espresso Dolce iced coffee concentrate frozen with milk and sugar and served as a coffee "slushee"—great on hot muggy days in New Orleans. Assorted pastries are available to go with the brew you choose.

P. J.'s is also located at Tulane and Loyola universities, 644 Camp St., 2727 Prytania St., and 637 N. Carrollton Ave.

Royal Blend Coffee & Tea House. 623 Royal St. ☎ **504/523-2716.** Pastry 75¢–$2.15; lunch $2.85–$4.95. Sun–Thurs 7am–8pm, Fri–Sat 7am–midnight. CAFE.

I'm not sure if I fell in love with this place because it's set back off the street and you walk through a courtyard to get to it or because the sparrows come in and eat crumbs off the floor. Order your light lunch (sandwiches, quiche, or salad) at the white tile-topped counter and take it out into the courtyard to eat or stay inside at a blue and white tiled table. If you're just in the mood for coffee and pastry, they've got plenty of that, too, and the pastry menu changes daily.

Royal Blend is also located at 222 Carondelet St. and at 244 Metairie Rd. in Metairie.

What to
in New Orleans

*I*n many respects the French Quarter *is* New Orleans—it's where it all began and is still the city's most popular sightseeing spot; many visitors never leave its confines. But I think that's a mistake. Exploring beyond the French Quarter will allow you to feel the pulse of the city's commerce, see river activities that keep the city alive, stroll through spacious parks, drive or walk by the impressive homes of the Garden District, and get a firsthand view of the bayou/lake connection that explains why New Orleans grew up here in the first place.

It won't take you long to find your way around, especially if you have armed yourself with the excellent map passed out by the **Tourist Commission,** 529 St. Ann St. (☎ **504/566-5031**).

At press time the Aquarium of the Americas had just completed an expansion, with the addition of its new IMAX theater (the first ever to be housed in an aquarium). The Audubon Institute was working on an expansion that will include a 16-acre riverfront park (stretching from the Governor Nicholls and Mandeville Street Wharves), an open-air museum, a themed playground, and a performance pavilion. The greatest feature of the new riverfront park will be the living science museum that will include an insectarium and a butterfly pavilion. The Audubon Institute expects to display close to a million species of insects. The insectarium and riverfront park are scheduled to open in late 1996. In addition, a brand-new baseball stadium for the city's minor league team, the New Orleans Zephyrs, has recently been completed. Plans are also underway for the building of other sports facilities around the city.

Remember not to allow the quaintness of the city to deaden your safety senses—New Orleans is a major metropolis, with the usual urban crime problems. Particular areas to steer clear of at night include the outer edges of the French Quarter, the Garden District, and the cemeteries. Try not to walk alone at night, and stay in well-lit, heavily trafficked areas—better yet, take a cab.

The narrow old streets of the French Quarter are lined with ancient buildings (many a century and a half old) whose fronts are embellished with that distinctive lacy ironwork. Their carriage drives or alleyways are often guarded by more ironwork in the form of massive gates; through them you can often catch glimpses of some of the loveliest courtyards in the world. Secluded from street noises and nosy neighbors, the courtyards provide beauty, relaxation, and privacy—three qualities that have always been important to New Orleanians—and ventilate the homes. Of course, many of these venerable buildings now serve as entertainment centers that often ring with merriment that is anything but restful; and many more now house shops of every description. But above ground level most also have apartments (many quite luxurious), keeping to the old-world custom of combining commercial ventures with living space. A few are still in the hands of original-owner families.

Thanks to the Vieux Carré Commission, not even "progress" is allowed to intrude on a heritage that blends gaiety with graciousness, the rowdiness of Bourbon Street with the quiet residential areas, and the busyness of commerce with the sense of leisure and goodwill. Progress is here, all right, with all its attendant benefits, but New Orleans insists that it conform to the city's traditional way of life, not the other way around. There's not even a traffic light within the whole of the French Quarter—they're relegated to fringe streets—and street lights are of the old gaslight style. Do not worry about those absent traffic lights—automobiles are banned from Royal and Bourbon streets during a good part of the day, making these streets pedestrian malls, and the area around Jackson Square is a permanent haven for foot traffic because no vehicles are allowed.

Laid out in 1718 in an almost perfect rectangle by a French royal engineer named Adrien de Pauger, the French Quarter is easy to get around. And even in these high-crime days, you're relatively safe wandering its streets during daylight hours. After dark, as in most metropolitan areas, it's best to exercise caution when walking alone outside the centers of activity—in New Orleans, that means Bourbon, Royal, and Chartres streets and the streets that connect them (there's safety as well as fun in the numbers that throng those streets all night long).

THE TOP SIGHTS

✪ **Aquarium of the Americas.** 1 Canal St. ☎ **504/861-2537.** Aquarium admission $10.50 adults, $8 seniors 65 and up, $5 children 2–12. IMAX

The French Quarter

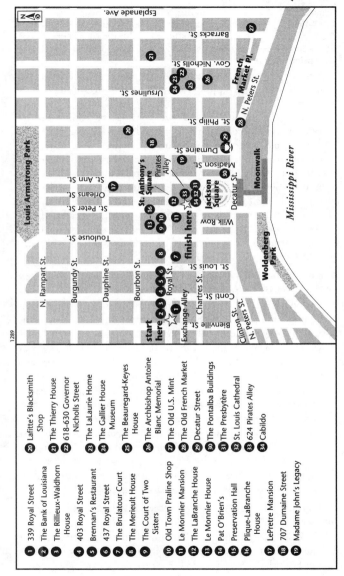

1289

- ① 339 Royal Street
- ② The Bank of Louisiana
- ③ The Rillieux-Waldhorn House
- ④ 403 Royal Street
- ⑤ Brennan's Restaurant
- ⑥ 437 Royal Street
- ⑦ The Brulatour Court
- ⑧ The Merieult House
- ⑨ The Court of Two Sisters
- ⑩ Old Town Praline Shop
- ⑪ Le Monnier Mansion
- ⑫ The LaBranche House
- ⑬ Le Monnier House
- ⑭ Pat O'Brien's
- ⑮ Preservation Hall
- ⑯ Plique-LaBranche House
- ⑰ LePretre Mansion
- ⑱ 707 Dumaine Street
- ⑲ Madame John's Legacy
- ⑳ Lafitte's Blacksmith Shop
- ㉑ The Thierry House
- ㉒ 618-630 Governor Nicholls Street
- ㉓ The LaLaurie Home
- ㉔ The Gallier House Museum
- ㉕ The Beauregard-Keyes House
- ㉖ The Archbishop Antoine Blanc Memorial
- ㉗ The Old U.S. Mint
- ㉘ The Old French Market
- ㉙ Decatur Street
- ㉚ The Pontalba Buildings
- ㉛ The Presbytère
- ㉜ St. Louis Cathedral
- ㉝ 624 Pirates Alley
- ㉞ Cabildo

admission $7.50 adults, $6.50 seniors, $5 children. Combination aquarium/
IMAX tickets $15 adults, $12 seniors, $9 children. Aquarium, Sun–Thurs
9:30am–6pm, Fri–Sat 9:30am–7pm. IMAX, Sun–Thurs 10am–6pm, Fri–Sat
10am–8pm. Shows every hour on the hour. Last ticket for admission sold one
hour before closing.

The one million-gallon Aquarium of the Americas is located on the
banks of the Mississippi River, right on the edge of the French
Quarter.

Five major exhibit areas and dozens of smaller aquarium displays
hold a wonderful collection of fish from North, Central, and South
America and are exhibited in environments that mimic their natural ones. You can take a walk through the underwater tunnel in the
Caribbean Reef exhibit and feel like you're swimming with the fish.
A re-creation of the Gulf of Mexico houses a sampling of fish that
you would see if you were swimming around in the Gulf—chances
are you'll think twice about that after you've seen the sharks! There's
also a wonderful tropical rain forest with piranha and tropical birds,
plus a penguin exhibit. The aquarium has just added a 350-seat
IMAX theater and a 12,000-square-foot changing exhibit gallery.

The Historic French Market. Decatur St. (just down from Jackson Square).
Farmer's Market open 24 hours daily; flea market open daily.

Legend has it that the French Market on Decatur Street, just down
from Jackson Square, was originally used by the Native Americans
as a bartering market. In 1812 it began to grow as an official market and in two later stages (one in 1822 and one in 1872) it was
expanded. Today you'll find all sorts of shops lining the street here.
Down toward the end there's a Farmer's Market where you can get
everything from fresh produce and fresh fish to hot sauces, Cajun/
Creole mixes, and beignet mix. The Farmer's Market also has a few
coffee and take-out stands, as well as souvenir shops.

The Flea Market, just a bit further down from the farmer's market, is a great place to shop for mementos and gifts for your friends
back home. T-shirts, jewelry, hats, belts, crystals, and sunglasses are
just some of the things you'll find as you browse among the tables
here. It's a good place to test your bargaining skills.

St. Louis Cathedral. 615 Père Antoine's Alley. ☎ **504/525-9585.** Free tours
Mon–Sat 9am–5pm, Sun 1:30–5pm.

The oldest active cathedral in the United States dominates Jackson
Square. This is actually the third building to stand on this spot. It
is of Spanish design, with a tower at each end and a higher central
tower, and its construction is of brick covered with stucco to protect the mortar from dampness. Inside, look for the six stained-glass

windows depicting the life of St. Louis (French King Louis IX), the cathedral's patron saint. There's also a spectacular painting on the wall above and behind the main altar, showing St. Louis proclaiming the Seventh Crusade from the steps of Notre Dame.

HISTORIC BUILDINGS

✪ **Old Absinthe House.** 240 Bourbon St. (2 blocks from Canal St.). ☎ **504/523-3181.** Free admission. Daily 10am–2am.

The Old Absinthe House was built in 1806 by two Spaniards and is still owned by their descendants (although they live in Spain and have nothing to do with running the place). The drink for which it was named is outlawed in this country now, but with a little imagination you can sip a modern-day libation and visualize Andrew Jackson and the Lafitte brothers plotting the desperate defense of New Orleans in 1815. It's the custom here to put your calling card on the wall, and the hundreds and hundreds of browning cards form a covering not unlike tattered wallpapers. It was a speakeasy during Prohibition, and when federal officers closed it in 1924, the interior was mysteriously stripped of its antique fixtures, including the long marble-topped bar and the old water dripper (used to drip water into absinthe), all of which just as mysteriously reappeared down the street at a corner establishment called, oddly enough, the Old Absinthe House Bar (400 Bourbon). It, too, follows the calling-card custom. If you can't keep all that straight, just remember that if you're in an Old Absinthe House that doesn't have entertainment, you're in the original *house*—if you see that grand brass water dripper on a marble-topped bar, you're in the new home of the original bar and fixtures.

Beauregard-Keyes House. 1113 Chartres St. ☎ **504/523-7257.** Admission $4 adults, $3 seniors and students, $1.50 children 12 and under. Mon–Sat 10am–3pm. Tours are offered on the hour.

This "raised cottage," with its Doric columns and handsome twin staircases, was built in 1826 by a wealthy New Orleans auctioneer, Joseph Le Carpentier. Confederate Gen. P. G. T. Beauregard lived in the house with several members of his family for 18 months between 1865 and 1867. From 1944 until 1970 it was the residence of Frances Parkinson Keyes, who wrote many novels about this region. One of them, *Madame Castel's Lodger,* is directly concerned with the general's stay in the house. *Dinner at Antoine's,* perhaps her most famous novel, also was written here. Mrs. Keyes left the house to a foundation, and the house, rear buildings, and garden are now open to the public.

Cabildo. 701 Chartres St. ☎ **504/568-6968.** Admission $4 adults, $3 students and seniors, children 12 and under free. Tues–Sun 9am–5pm.

On Jackson Square, the Cabildo is the site of the signing of the Louisiana Purchase Transfer. Reopened in 1994 following an extensive restoration in the wake of a fire, the National Historic Landmark now houses a comprehensive new exhibit that traces Louisiana's past from exploration through the Civil War and Reconstruction from a multicultural perspective.

Gallier House Museum. 1132 Royal St. ☎ **504/523-6722.** Admission $4 adults, $3 seniors and students, $2.25 children 5–11, children under 5 free. Mon–Sat 10am–4:30pm, Sun noon–4:30pm. Last tour begins at 4pm.

The Gallier House Museum was built by James Gallier Jr. as his residence in 1857. The carefully restored town house contains an early working bathroom, a passive ventilation system, and furnishings of the period. The adjoining building houses historical exhibits, as well as films on decorative plaster work, ornamental ironwork, woodgraining, and marbling.

Old Ursuline Convent. 1114 Chartres St. ☎ **504/529-3040.** Admission $4 adults, $2 students and seniors, children under 8 free. Tours Tues–Fri 10 and 11am and 1, 2, and 3pm; Sat–Sun 11:15am, 1, and 2pm.

Across from the Beauregard-Keyes House is the Archbishop Antoine Blanc Memorial, which includes the Old Ursuline Convent. The Sisters of Ursula were for years the only teachers and nurses in New Orleans—they established the first schools for Catholic girls, for African Americans, and for Native Americans, and they set up the first orphanage in Louisiana. The nuns moved out of the convent in 1824 (they're in an uptown location these days), and in 1831 the state legislature met here. It now houses Catholic archives dating from 1718. Especially noteworthy is the fact that this is the oldest building of record not only in New Orleans but also in the entire Mississippi Valley, and it is the only surviving building from the French colonial effort in what is now the United States. Included in the complex is the beautiful restored old Chapel of the Archbishops, erected in 1845 and still used as a house of worship.

The Old U.S. Mint. 400 Esplanade Ave. ☎ **504/568-6968.** Admission $4 adults, $3 seniors and students, children under 12 free. Tues–Sun 9am–5pm.

The Old U.S. Mint houses exhibits on New Orleans jazz and on the city's Carnival celebrations. These displays contain a comprehensive collection of pictures, musical instruments, and other artifacts connected with jazz greats—Louis Armstrong's first trumpet is here.

Across the hall there's a stunning array of Carnival mementos, from ornate Mardi Gras costumes to a street scene complete with maskers and a parade float. Entrances to the Mint are on both Esplanade Avenue and Barracks Street.

Pontalba Apartments. In the 1850 House, 523 St. Ann St. ☎ **504/568-6968.** Admission $4 adults, $3 seniors and students, children 12 and under free. Tues–Sun 10am–5pm.

These historic apartments are located in the Lower Pontalba Buildings, in a restored house of the period. They're authentically furnished from parlor to kitchen to servants' quarters.

Presbytère. 751 Chartres St. ☎ **504/568-6968.** Admission $4 adults, $3 seniors and students, children 12 and under free. Tues–Sun 9am–5pm.

Located on Jackson Square, the Presbytère was planned as housing for the clergy but was never used for that purpose. It exhibits the paintings of Louisianan artists as well as displays on local history and culture.

Spring Fiesta Historic House. 826 St. Ann St. ☎ **504/945-0322** (call 504/581-1367 on Fri). $4 donation requested. By appointment only.

This historic mid–19th-century town house is owned by the New Orleans Spring Fiesta Association. It is furnished with lovely antiques of the Victorian era and many outstanding objets d'art from New Orleans's golden age of the 1800s.

MUSEUMS

In addition to the museums listed here, you might be interested in visiting the **Germaine Wells Mardi Gras Museum,** at 813 Bienville St. (on the second floor of Antoine's Restaurant), where you'll find a private collection of Mardi Gras costumes and ball gowns dating from around 1910 to 1960. Admission is free, and the museum is open during restaurant hours.

✪ **Historic New Orleans Collection—Museum/Research Center.** 533 Royal St. ☎ **504/523-4662.** Free admission. Tours $2, given Tues–Sat at 10 and 11am and 2 and 3pm. Wheelchair accommodation is available. Tues–Sat 10am–4:45pm. Closed major holidays and Mardi Gras.

The Historic New Orleans Collection is located within a complex of historic French Quarter buildings. The oldest, constructed in the late 18th century, is one of the few structures to escape the disastrous fire of 1794. Today, the collection serves the public as a museum and research center for state and local history with history-related gifts in the shop. The Williams Gallery, free to the public, presents changing exhibitions that focus on Louisiana's history and culture.

New Orleans Attractions

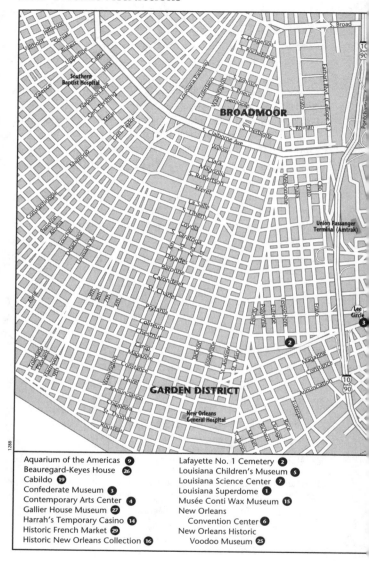

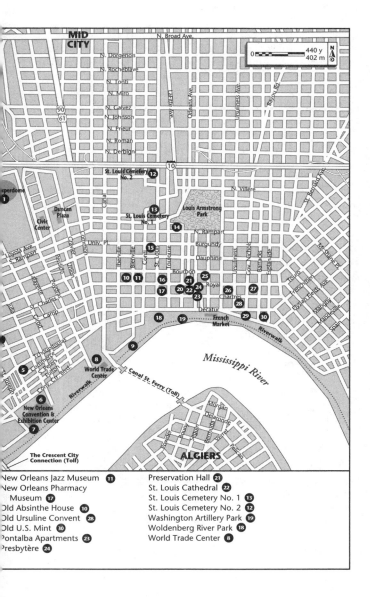

New Orleans Jazz Museum ⑪
New Orleans Pharmacy
  Museum ⑰
Old Absinthe House ⑩
Old Ursuline Convent ㉘
Old U.S. Mint ㉚
Pontalba Apartments ㉓
Presbytère ㉔

Preservation Hall ㉑
St. Louis Cathedral ㉒
St. Louis Cemetery No. 1 ⑬
St. Louis Cemetery No. 2 ⑫
Washington Artillery Park ⑲
Woldenberg River Park ⑱
World Trade Center ⑧

Guided tours are available of both the founders' residence, one of the "hidden" houses of the Vieux Carré, and the Louisiana History Galleries. The History Gallery Tour is a must for all visitors who would like to learn more about Louisiana's colorful and exciting past.

Musée Conti Wax Museum. 917 Conti St. ☎ **504/525-2605.** Admission $5.75 adults, $5.25 seniors over 62, $3.50 children 4–17, children under 4 are free. Daily 10am–5pm. Closed Christmas and Mardi Gras Day.

This museum offers New Orleans history depicted by life-size wax figures with authentic costumes and settings of Louisiana legends (Andrew Jackson, Jean Lafitte, Huey Long, Louis Armstrong, and Pete Fountain), plus an added "Haunted Dungeon" illustrating well-known horror tales. You'll also be able to see fabulous Mardi Gras Indian costumes.

✪ **New Orleans Historic Voodoo Museum.** 724 Dumaine St. ☎ **504/522-5223.** Admission $5 adults, $4 students and seniors. French Quarter tour $18 per person, cemetery tour $10 per person. Daily 10am–dusk.

If tales of Marie Laveau have captured your imagination, you'll definitely want to stop by the Voodoo Museum, in the heart of the Vieux Carré. The dark, musty interior seems exactly the right setting for artifacts of the occult from all over the globe and a fitting place in which to learn more of that curious mixture of African and Catholic religions and rituals brought to New Orleans in the late 1700s by former Santo Domingan slaves.

There's a guided voodoo walking tour of the French Quarter that leaves the museum at 1pm daily and visits Congo Square (now Beauregard Square) and a pharmacy displaying voodoo potions. There is another tour that leaves at 1:30pm and takes you on a visit to Marie Laveau's reputed grave. The museum can arrange psychic readings and visits to voodoo rituals if you want to delve deeper into this subject, which has bedeviled New Orleans for centuries.

New Orleans Pharmacy Museum. 514 Chartres St. ☎ **504/565-8027.** Admission $2 adults, $1 seniors and students, children under 12 are admitted free. Tues–Sun 10am–5pm.

Founded in 1950, the New Orleans Pharmacy Museum is an interesting stop on a tour of the French Quarter. In 1823 the first licensed pharmacist in the United States, Louis J. Dufilho Jr. opened an apothecary shop here at 514 Chartres St. The Creole-style town house doubled as his home, and in the interior courtyard he cultivated the herbs he would need for fabricating his medicines. Inside the museum you'll find old apothecary bottles, pill tile, and suppository molds as well as the old glass cosmetics counter (pharmacists of the 1800s also manufactured make-up and perfumes). There's even an 1855 black-and-rose Italian marble soda fountain.

PARKS

Washington Artillery Park. Between Jackson Square and the Mississippi River. ☎ **504/529-5284.** Free admission. Dawn to dusk.

Just past Jackson Brewery, pretty riverside Washington Artillery Park, with its splashing fountains, has always been a "promenade" for New Orleanians, and now the elevated area has been renamed the Moon Walk (for Mayor "Moon" Landrieu). There are attractive plantings and benches from which to view the city's main industry—its busy port (second only to Amsterdam for tonnage handled each year). To your right you will see the Greater New Orleans Bridge and the World Trade Center of New Orleans (formerly the International Trade Mart) skyscraper, as well as the Toulouse Street wharf, departure point for excursion steamboats.

Woldenberg River Park. Along the Mississippi River in the French Quarter. ☎ **504/861-2537.** Free admission. Dawn to dusk.

Some 13 acres of the riverfront, from Canal Street to St. Peter Street, have been converted into the Woldenberg River Park. This oasis of greenery in the heart of the city is centered by a large lawn, with a brick promenade leading to the Mississippi and more than 600 trees—oaks, magnolias, willows, and crape myrtles—and 1,400 shrubs to beautify this tranquil spot. The park is now the setting for the Aquarium of the Americas (see above).

2 Outside the French Quarter

UPTOWN & THE GARDEN DISTRICT

Outside the borders of the French Quarter lies "American" New Orleans. It came into being because of Creole snobbery. You see, those semiaristocratic French Quarter natives had no use for the crass Americans who came flooding into the city after the 1803 Louisiana Purchase, so they presented a united and closed front to keep "their" New Orleans exclusive. Not to be outdone, the newcomers simply bought up land in what had been the old Gravier plantation upriver from Canal Street and set about building their New Orleans. Exhibiting the celebrated Yankee flair for enterprise, they very soon dominated the business scene, centered on Canal Street itself, and constructed mansions different from the traditional Quarter residences but surrounded by beautiful gardens. In 1833 what we now know as the Garden District was incorporated as Lafayette City, and—thanks in large part to the New Orleans–Carrollton Railroad, which covered the route of today's St. Charles Avenue trolley—the Americans kept right on expanding until they reached the tiny resort town of Carrollton. It wasn't until 1852 that the various sections came together officially to become a united New Orleans.

✪ **Superdome.** 1500 block of Poydras St. ☎ **504/587-3810** for tour information. Hourly guided tours daily between 10am–4pm (except during Superdome events). Tour prices $6 adults, $5 seniors, $4 children ages 5–10; children under 5 admitted free.

As tall as a 27-story building, the colossal Louisiana Superdome, with a seating capacity of 76,000, is a windowless structure whose computerized climate-control system uses more than 9,000 *tons* of equipment. It is one of the largest buildings in the world in diameter (680 feet), and its grounds cover some 13 acres. Inside, no posts obstruct the view for spectator sports such as football, baseball, and basketball, and movable partitions and seats give it the flexibility to form the best configuration for almost any event. Most people think of the Superdome as a sports center only, but this big flying saucer of a building plays host to conventions, trade shows, and large theatrical and musical productions as well. Entertainment and instant replays are provided via two Diamond Vision screens.

BAYOU ST. JOHN & LAKE PONTCHARTRAIN

Bayou St. John is one of the most important reasons New Orleans is where it is today. When Jean-Baptiste Le Moyne, sieur de Bienville, was commissioned to establish a settlement that would protect the mouth of the Mississippi River for the French Crown against British expansion, he recognized the strategic importance of the "back-door" access to the Gulf of Mexico provided by the bayou's linkage to Lake Pontchartrain. Boats could enter the lake from the Gulf, then follow the bayou to within easy portage distance of the mouth of the Mississippi River. Native American tribes had used this route for years, and Bienville was quick to see its advantages.

The path from city to bayou back in those early days is today's Bayou Road, an extension of Governor Nicholls Street in the French Quarter. The modern-day Gentilly Boulevard, which crosses the bayou, was another Native American trail—it led around the lake and on to settlements in Florida after a relatively short boat trip.

As the new town grew and prospered, planters moved out along the shores of the bayou, and in the early 1800s a canal was dug to connect the waterway with the city. It reached a basin at the edge of Congo Square. The lake itself became a popular recreation area, with fine restaurants and dance halls (as well as meeting places for voodoo practitioners, who held secret ceremonies along its shores). Gradually the city reached out beyond the French Quarter and enveloped the whole area—farmlands, plantation homes, and resorts. So on your exploration of this part of New Orleans, you'll see traces of that development. The canal is gone, filled in long ago, and the bayou itself is no longer navigable (even if it were, bridges were built too low to permit the passage of boats of any size), but residents still prize their waterfront sites, and rowboats and sailboats make use of the bayou's surface.

The simplest way to reach the Bayou St. John from the French Quarter is to drive straight out Esplanade Avenue about 20 blocks. Just before you reach the bayou, you'll pass St. Louis Cemetery No. 3 (it's just past Leda Street), at which rest many prominent New Orleanians—among them are Thomy Lafon, the black philanthropist who bought the old Orleans Ballroom as an orphanage for African American children and thus put an end to its infamous "quadroon balls," and Father Adrien Rouquette, who lived and worked among the Choctaw. Just past the cemetery, Esplanade reaches Moss Street, and a left turn will put you on that street, which runs along the banks of Bayou St. John.

Drive along Wisner Boulevard, along the bank of Bayou St. John, and you'll pass some of New Orleans's grandest modern homes, which provide a sharp contrast to those over on Moss Street. Stay on Wisner to Robert E. Lee Boulevard, turn right, and drive to Elysian Fields Avenue, then turn left. That's Louisiana State University's New Orleans campus on your left (its main campus is in Baton Rouge).

Turn left onto the broad concrete highway that is Lakeshore Drive. It runs for $5^{1}/_{2}$ miles along the lake, and in summer the parkway alongside its seawall is usually swarming with swimmers and picnickers. On the other side are more luxurious, ultramodern residences.

Lake Pontchartrain itself is some 40 miles long and 25 miles wide. Native Americans once lived along its shores on both sides, and it was a major waterway long before white people were seen in this hemisphere. You can drive across it over the Greater New Orleans Causeway, the $23^{3}/_{4}$-mile-long bridge, the longest in the world.

"See Naples and die," says the proverb. My view of things is that you should see Canal Street, New Orleans, and then try to live as much longer as ever you can.

—G. A. Sala, *America Revisited,* 1882

When you cross the mouth of the Bayou St. John, you'll be where the old Spanish Fort was built in 1770. Its remains are now nestled amidst elegant modern homes. In the early 1800s there was a light-house here, and in the 1820s a railroad brought New Orleanians out to a hotel, a casino, a bandstand, bathing houses, and restaurants that made this a popular resort area.

Look for the Mardi Gras fountain on your left. Bronze plaques around its base are inscribed with the names of Mardi Gras krewes, and if you time your lake visit to coincide with sundown, you'll see the fountain beautifully lit in Mardi Gras colors of purple (for justice), green (for faith), and gold (for power).

Down at the end of Lakeshore Drive, when you come to the old, white, coast guard lighthouse, you'll know you've reached West End. This is an interesting little park that's home to several yacht clubs, a marina, and restaurants, many of which have been here for years and look just like lakeside restaurants should (not too fancy—more interested in the view out over the water and good eating than in "decorator-style" interiors). This old fishing community has, over the years, become the main pleasure-boating center of New Orleans, and the Southern Yacht Club here was established in 1840, making it the second oldest in the country. After the railroad began bringing pleasure-seekers here from the city in the 1870s, showboats and floating circuses would often pull up and dock for waterside perfor-mances. West End is an excellent place to stop for a bite to eat, if indeed it isn't your destination when you set out for the lakeside with a fresh seafood dinner in mind.

To reach Buckstown, which lines the bank of a narrow canal behind the restaurants on the western side of West End park, turn to the left on Lakeshore Drive at the coast guard station, then turn right on Lake Avenue (it's the first street you come to). Buckstown is another small fishing community that still retains its old-time atmosphere. There are also many good seafood restaurants here.

CEMETERIES

In the beginning, burials were made along the banks of the Mississippi, but when the little settlement of New Orleans began to grow, more cemetery space was a necessity. However, there was a big problem: The soggy ground was so damp that graves would fill with water even before the coffins could be lowered. To solve that problem aboveground tombs were constructed. The coffin would be put in place on the ground, walls of brick would be built around it, and then the walls would be plastered and whitewashed. The entrances to the tombs were closed by marble tablets, and many were enclosed with iron fences. Some were even finished off with rounded roofs or topped with eaves—like tiny, windowless houses. It is easy to see why the cemeteries came to be called "Cities of the Dead," because they are arranged along narrow paths, many of which have "street" names. These miniature cities even have their "skyscrapers," since upper floors would be added as members of the same family passed away and were entombed right on top of the existing vault. Along the outer walls of the cemeteries, you'll see rows of wall vaults, or "ovens," which hold the remains of the city's poor. Incidentally, you may be perplexed by the long list of names for just one tomb—that's because, to economize on space, New Orleanians use the same tomb over and over, simply moving the old remains to a lower level after two years have passed and interring a fresh body in the vacated space.

St. Louis Cemetery No. 1, in the 400 block of Basin Street, was the first, established in the 1740s; you may be familiar with it through the film *Easy Rider*. Marie Laveau I spends eternity here— followers mark her grave located just a few steps from the Basin Street entrance with red crosses. **St. Louis Cemetery No. 2** is a few blocks away down from Conti Street on Claiborne Avenue (from Iberville to St. Louis streets). If you see one of the unmarked "ovens" with red crosses on its concrete slab, that's the place where Marie Laveau II, daughter of the original voodoo queen, may be resting from her voodoo activities (though almost all other Protestant and Catholic cemeteries in town also claim to house her remains). It seems that no matter how many times the slab is painted over, the faithful keep coming back to mark it and ask Marie's favors. **Lafayette No. 1 Cemetery** is in the Garden District bounded by Washington, Prytania, and Coliseum streets. Perhaps the most beautiful of all is **Metairie Cemetery,** at the intersection of

Pontchartrain Boulevard and Metairie Road—and it wouldn't be here at all except for one New Orleanian's pique at being denied admission to the exclusive Metairie Jockey Club at the racetrack that once operated on these grounds. He was an American who, to strike back at those uppity Creoles who wouldn't let him in, bought up the land, turned it into a burial ground, and swore that from then on only the dead would gain admittance.

Before leaving this subject, I must add one word of warning. Because a lot of crime has been associated with the cemeteries, particularly St. Louis Cemeteries No. 1 and No. 2, it is best not to walk in them alone. Join one of the walking tours listed under "Organized Tours," later in this chapter, if you're interested in viewing the tombs up close.

CHURCHES

Sometimes people don't realize that St. Louis Cathedral (see "The French Quarter," above) isn't the only church in New Orleans. Below, you'll find a few others that you might want to stop in and have a look at.

St. Alphonsus Church. 2029 Constance St. ☎ 504/522-6748.

The Irish built St. Alphonsus Church in 1855, and the gallery and columns may vaguely remind you of the St. Louis Cathedral in the French Quarter. A beloved Redemptorist priest, Fr. Francis Xavier Seeles, is buried in the church. He is credited with the working of many miracles; if you visit the church, you're likely to see letters of petition on his tomb.

St. Patrick's Church. 724 Camp St. ☎ 504/525-4413.

St. Patrick's was founded in a tiny wooden building to serve Irish Catholics in the parish. The present building, begun in 1838, was constructed around the old one, which was then dismantled inside the new building. The distinguished architect James Gallier Sr. designed much of the interior, including the altar. It opened in 1840, proudly proclaimed as the "American" Catholics' answer to the St. Louis Cathedral in the French Quarter (where, according to the Americans, God spoke only in French).

Church of St. John the Baptist. 1139 Dryades St. ☎ 504/525-1726.

Because you wouldn't be human if you didn't wonder about that gilded dome so prominent against the skyline (especially as you drive on the elevated expressway), I'm including the Church of St. John the Baptist. It was built by the Irish in 1871, and its most noteworthy features (besides the exceptional brickwork of the exterior) are the beautiful stained-glass windows crafted by artists in Munich, and the Stations of the Cross and sacristy murals that were painted during and after World War II by Belgian artist Dom Gregory Dewit.

Our Lady of Guadalupe International Shrine of St. Jude. 411 N. Rampart St. ☎ **504/525-1551.**

Located on the corner of Rampart and Conti streets, this building was put up in 1826 as a chapel convenient to the St. Louis Cemetery No. 1—funeral services were held here rather than in St. Louis Cathedral so as not to spread disease within the confines of the Quarter, and it became known as the "Burial Chapel." In the intervening years it has been renovated, and it now houses an International Shrine of St. Jude (the saint of impossible causes, she is often thanked publicly for favors in the "Personals" column of the *Times-Picayune*). Another saint is honored here by a statue next to the main altar. His name is St. Expedite, a name that legend says was given to the statue when it arrived at the church in a packing crate with no identification but stamped "Expedite."

HISTORIC BUILDINGS

Pitot House. 1440 Moss St. ☎ **504/482-0312.** Admission $3 adults, $2 seniors, $1 children under 12. Wed–Sat 10am–3pm.

The Pitot House is a typical West Indies–style plantation home, restored and furnished with Louisianan and American antiques dating from the early 1800s. Dating from 1799, it originally stood where the nearby modern Catholic school is now. In 1810 it became the home of James Pitot, the first mayor of incorporated New Orleans, and it is now known by his name. It has wide galleries on the sides and large columns supporting the second floor.

Jackson Barracks. 6400 St. Claude Ave. ☎ **504/271-6262,** ext. 242, or 504/278-6242. Free admission. Mon–Fri 7:30am–3:30pm.

On an extension of Rampart Street downriver from the French Quarter is this series of fine old brick buildings with white columns. They were built in 1834–35 for troops who were stationed at the river forts. Some say Andrew Jackson, who never quite trusted New Orleans Creoles, planned the barracks to be as secure against attack from the city as from outside forces. The barracks now serve as headquarters for the Louisiana National Guard, and there's a marvelous military museum in the old powder magazine, which has an extensive collection of military items that span the American wars. It's best to call before you go to confirm that the barracks and museum are open. The museum recently underwent an expansion, and the complex now consists of the original powder magazine and a new annex that holds exhibits from World War II to Operation Desert Storm.

MUSEUMS & GALLERIES

Confederate Museum. 929 Camp St. ☎ **504/523-4522.** Admission $4 adults, $2 children under 12. Mon–Sat 10am–4pm.

Located not far from the French Quarter, the Confederate Museum was established in 1899, close enough to the end of the Civil War for many donations to be in better condition than is sometimes true of museum items. There are battle flags, weapons, personal effects of Confederate President Jefferson Davis (including his evening clothes), part of Robert E. Lee's silver camp service, and many portraits of Confederate military and civilian personalities.

✪ **Contemporary Arts Center.** 900 Camp St. ☎ **504/523-1216.** Admission $3 general, $2 students and seniors, free to members. Admission is free to all on Thurs. Performance prices range from $3–$15. Mon–Sat 10am–5pm, Sun 11am–5pm.

Located outside the French Quarter, in what used to be the warehouse district and is now the Arts District, the Contemporary Arts Center exhibits the artwork of regional, national, and international artists. The CAC also presents theater, performance art, dance, and music concerts. Exhibitions change every six to eight weeks, and performances are weekly.

✪ **New Orleans Museum of Art.** In City Park, Lelong Ave. ☎ **504/488-2631.** Admission $6 adults, $3 seniors and children, free to all on Thurs. Tues–Sun 10am–5pm.

This museum is in a neoclassical building housing pre-Columbian, Renaissance, and contemporary art exhibited to show the history of art development. The columned main building is a beauty inside and out. Its first-floor Delgado Great Hall leads to a branched staircase at the back that rises to a mezzanine overlooking the hall. Notice, too, the bronze statue of Hercules as an archer just outside the entrance. The original building, about 80 years old, has been expanded by the addition of three wings, and the art inside does justice to its housing. There's a lovely portrait of Estelle Musson, a relative of the French impressionist painter Edgar Degas, who painted this likeness on one of his visits to the city. The 22 sections

of the Kress Renaissance collection, pre-Columbian art, an
by Rodin mix well with 20th-century art. NOMA recently
went a $23 million expansion project that created more gallery sp
for portions of the museum's collection (both western and non
western art from the pre-Christian era to the present) that had
previously been relegated to storage. In addition, there is now an
entire floor devoted to nonwestern and ethnographic art, including
Asian, African, pre-Columbian, Oceanic, and Native American art.

AN INSIDER'S LOOK AT MARDI GRAS

✪ **Blaine Kern's Mardi Gras World.** 223 Newton St., Algiers Point.
☎ **504/361-7821.** Admission $5.50 adults, $4.50 seniors, $3.25 children.
Daily 9:30am–4:30pm. Closed on Mardi Gras, Easter Sunday, Thanksgiving, and
Christmas. Take the Canal Street Ferry, which is free, across the river. The ride
takes about 10 minutes. Look for the free shuttle that will take you from the
dock to Mardi Gras World. The last ferry returns at around 11:15pm. Check
schedule before you set out.

When I was a kid, Mardi Gras floats fascinated me. I marveled at
their elaborate detail and I wondered who could possibly create such
incredible works of art. Well, now I know, and you will, too, if you
make the trip to Blaine Kern's Mardi Gras World, where you can
see floats being made year-round. Take one of the tours and you'll
get to see sculptors at work, first making small "sketches" of the figures and then finally creating and painting the enormous sculptures
that adorn Mardi Gras floats each year. A film about Mardi Gras is
presented, and you can even get a souvenir picture taken—dress up
in Mardi Gras costumes or have it taken with one of the colossal
float figures.

A PANORAMA

World Trade Center of New Orleans. 2 Canal St. ☎ **504/581-4888.**
Admission $2 adults, $1 children 6–12, children under 6 free. Daily 9am–5pm.

Down at the river, the World Trade Center of New Orleans is the
center of the city's maritime industry as well as the home of most
international consulates. On the 31st floor there's an observation
deck that looks out onto the city and the harbor scene. For a stunning ride up, use the outside elevator. The observation deck, called
Viewpoint, is open every day except Christmas, Mardi Gras, and
Thanksgiving. This is truly an incomparable view. There are high-
power telescopes to zoom in on your favorite site for only 25¢. For
more relaxed viewing, go on up to the 33rd-floor revolving cocktail
lounge.

n both Loyola and Tulane, Audubon Park
reaching from St. Charles Avenue all the way
the Mississippi. This tract of land once belonged to Jean-Baptiste
Le Moyne, the founder of New Orleans, and later was part of the
Etienne de Bore plantation. The city purchased it in 1871; a golf
course now lies on the section where the World's Industrial and
Cotton Centennial Exposition was held in 1884–85. In spite of having what was then the largest building in the world (33 acres under
one roof) as its main exhibition hall, the exposition was such a
financial disaster that everything except a horticultural hall had
to be sold off. (The Horticultural Hall fell victim to a hurricane a
little later.) After that, serious work was begun to make this into a
park. Although John James Audubon, our country's best-known
ornithologist, lived only briefly in New Orleans (in a cottage on
Dauphine Street in the French Quarter—his studio was located on
Barracks Street), the city has honored his contributions in the nam-
ing of both Audubon Park and Audubon Zoo.

The huge trees with black bark you see here are live oaks, and
some go back to the days when this was a plantation. They're ever-
greens and shed only once a year, in early spring. Their spreading
limbs turn walkways into covered alleys, and there are winding lagoons, fountains, and statuary, as well as a very nice zoo (see later
in this section). Scattered about are gazebos, shelters, and playground
areas—and that funny-looking mound over near the river, actually
in the zoo, is called "Monkey Hill," constructed so that the children
of this flatland city could see what a hill looked like. The pavilion
on the riverbank is one of the most pleasant places from which to
view the Mississippi.

There's an 18-hole golf course in the front half, picnic facilities,
tennis courts, a 1.8-mile jogging track, 18 exercise stations, and
horseback riding. The Audubon Zoo is toward the back of the park.

When you reach the end of St. Charles Avenue (where the streetcar turns onto Carrollton Avenue), the green hill over by the river
is the levee—if the water happens to be high enough, you'll see the
tops of ships as they pass by.

Note: In spite of the fact that the park is open until 10pm, it is
not advisable to be there after it gets dark.

✪ **City Park.** 1 Dreyfous Ave. ☎ **504/483-9358.** Free admission. Daily
6am–7pm.

Right at the entrance is a statue of Gen. P. G. T. Beauregard, whose order to fire on Fort Sumter opened the Civil War and whom New Orleanians fondly call the "Great Creole." The park was once part of the Louis Allard plantation, and the huge old oaks looked down on a favorite pastime in New Orleans during the 1700s: dueling.

The extensive, beautifully landscaped grounds hold a botanical gardens and conservatory, four golf courses, picnic areas, a restaurant, lagoons for boating and fishing, tennis courts, horses for hire for the lovely trails, a bandstand, two miniature trains, and Children's Storyland (see "Especially for Kids" in this chapter for more details), an amusement area with a carousel ride for children. You'll also find the New Orleans Museum of Art on Lelong Avenue in City Park in a building that is itself a work of art (see "Museums and Galleries" earlier in this chapter for more details).

Chalmette National Historical Park. 8608 West St. Bernard Hwy. ☎ **504/ 589-4430.** Free admission. Daily 8:30am–5pm. To reach the park, continue on St. Claude Avenue until it becomes St. Bernard Highway. The park will be on your right.

On these grounds the bloody Battle of New Orleans was waged on January 14, 1815. Ironically, the battle should never have been fought at all, since the War of 1812 had by then been concluded by a treaty signed two weeks before in Ghent, Belgium. The treaty was not, however, in effect, and word had simply never reached Congress, the commander of the British forces, or Andrew Jackson, who stood with American forces to defend New Orleans and the mouth of the Mississippi River. The battle did, however, succeed in bringing New Orleanians together more than they had ever been and in making Andrew Jackson a hero forever in this city.

You can visit the battleground and see markers that will let you follow the course of the battle in detail. In the Beauregard plantation house on the grounds, you will find interesting exhibits, and the Visitor Center presents a film and other exhibits on the battle. There also is a National Cemetery here, which was established in 1864; it holds only two American veterans of the Battle of New Orleans, but some 14,000 Union soldiers who fell in the Civil War are buried here. For a really terrific view of the Mississippi River, climb the levee in back of the Beauregard House.

Joe Brown Memorial Park (& the Louisiana Nature Center). Nature Center Dr., New Orleans East. ☎ **504/244-4663** or 504/246-5672. Admission $4 adults, $3 seniors, $2 children. Tues–Fri 9am–5pm, Sat 10am–5pm, Sun noon–5pm.

Part of the Audubon Institute, Joe Brown Park is an 86-acre tract of Louisiana forest where guided walks are given daily (except Monday). Weekdays a nature film is shown, and weekends offer additional activities as well (canoeing, bird-watching, arts and crafts workshops, and others). Three miles of trails are available for public use. There is a wheelchair-accessible raised wooden walkway for shorter walks. The Louisiana Nature Center offers changing exhibits and hands-on activities. There is a planetarium with shows on Saturday and Sunday, and on Friday and Saturday nights there are laser rock shows. Call 504/246-STAR for the current planetarium schedule. To get there, take I-10 to Exit 244; pass the Plaza Shopping Center and make a left onto Nature Center Drive.

Longue Vue House & Gardens. 7 Bamboo Rd. ☎ **504/488-5488.** Admission $7 adults, $6 seniors, $3 children and students. Mon–Sat 10am–4:30pm, Sun 1–5pm. Closed New Year's Day, Mardi Gras, July 4, Labor Day, Thanksgiving, and Christmas Day.

Just off Metairie Road, you'll find the lovely, eight-acre Longue Vue Estate, one of the most beautiful garden settings in this area. The mansion is built in the classical tradition. As with the great country houses of England, it was designed to foster a close rapport between indoors and outdoors, with vistas of formal terraces and pastoral woods. Some parts of the enchanting gardens were inspired by those of the Sultans' summerhouse, the Generalife, in Granada, Spain; besides the colorful flowering plants, there are formal boxwood parterres, fountains, and a colonnaded loggia. Highlights are the Canal Garden; Walled Garden; Wild Garden (which features native iris); and Spanish Court (with pebbled walkways, fountains, and changing horticultural displays).

A DAY AT THE ZOO

✪ **Audubon Zoo.** 6500 Magazine St. ☎ **504/861-5101.** Admission $8 adults, $4 seniors 65 and older and children 2–12. Admission to the Butterflies in Flight exhibit is $2 additional. Daily 9:30am–5:30pm (the zoo remains open until 6pm on Sat and Sun in summer). The last ticket is sold 1 hour before closing. Closed holidays.

The Audubon Zoo is one of the top five zoos in the country. Here, in a setting of subtropical plantings, waterfalls, and lagoons, some 1,800 animals (including rare and endangered species) live in natural habitats. Don't plan to spend less than two or three hours—more if you have time to spare—in this delightful oasis of animal culture. The new Butterflies in Flight exhibit is a glorious butterfly garden replete with lush, colorful vegetation. It houses more than 1,000 butterflies as well as a pupae hatchery. A terrific way to visit is to arrive on the sternwheeler *John James Audubon* and depart via the St. Charles streetcar, which is reached by way of a lovely stroll through Audubon Park or on a complimentary shuttle bus. During your visit to the zoo look for the bronze statue of John James Audubon. It's in a grove of trees and the naturalist is shown with a notebook and pencil in hand.

3   Especially for Kids

New Orleans is a great place for kids, and there's so much for a child to learn in a city filled with history. Below I've listed some places I think your kids might enjoy (chances are that you will, too). In addition to the attractions listed below, **Accents on Arrangements,** 938 Lafayette St., no. 410 (☎ **504/524-1227**), also offers tours specially designed to meet the needs and interests of children.

All kids love the **French Market** because it's small and there's so much to see. Take them on a horse-and-buggy ride around the **Vieux Carré:** You'll all learn about the fascinating and amusing history of the city. Of course, the **Riverfront streetcar** and **a ferry ride on the Mississippi** are fun—you can get them to imagine that they're playing a part in the lives of Huck Finn and Tom Sawyer. Finish it off with a visit to **Aquarium of the Americas** (see "The French Quarter" earlier in this chapter).

Some children might like a visit to a museum or two, and I'd suggest the **Confederate Museum,** the **New Orleans Historic Voodoo Museum,** or the **Musée Conti Wax Museum**—all with complete listings earlier in this chapter.

If they're getting restless being inside so much and the weather is nice, take them to one of the parks listed above and have a picnic lunch.

Below I've listed a couple of things that are absolutely child oriented and are worth a visit.

✪ **Louisiana Children's Museum.** 420 Julia St. ☎ **504/523-1357.** Admission $5. Tues–Sat 9:30am–5pm, Sun noon–5pm. Mon June–Aug, 9:30am–5pm.

People of all ages will delight in exploring more than 45,000 square feet of dynamic "hands-on" exhibits—it's not your ordinary playhouse! Visitors might play and meet new friends in the toddler area, explore the powers of math and physics through the 45 exhibits in "The Lab"; or take in a performance in science, drama, dance, art, or puppetry in the Times-Picayune Theatre.

Children's Storyland. In City Park. ☎ **504/483-9381.** Admission $1.50 children and adults, children under 2 free. Wed–Fri 10am–12:30pm, Sat–Sun 10am–4:30pm, except Jan and Feb when it's only open on Sat and Sun.

This is an enchanted playground where youngsters can slide down Jack and Jill's hill, climb Little Miss Muffet's spiderweb, or have an imaginary sword fight on Captain Hook's pirate ship. Larger than life fairy-tale figures such as Puss-n-Boots, Rapunzel, and Jack (of Beanstalk fame) will delight young children. It's right across from the tennis courts on Victory Avenue.

4 Organized Tours

In addition to the tours detailed below, another marvelous way to view the city is from the riverboats that cruise the harbor and a little stretch of the Mississippi River. Docks are at the foot of Toulouse and Canal streets, and there's ample parking for the car while you sit back and relax on the water. Reservations are required for all these tours; the prices quoted here are subject to change.

There's an excellent walking tour offered by the nonprofit volunteer group **Friends of the Cabildo** (☎ **504/523-3939**). This tour furnishes guides for a two-hour, on-foot exploration that will provide a good overview of the area. Leaving from in front of the Museum Store, 523 St. Ann St., your guide will "show and tell" you about most of the Quarter's historic buildings' exteriors and the interiors of selected Louisiana State Museum buildings. You're asked to pay a donation of $10 per adult, $5 for seniors over 65 and children from 13 to 20 (those 12 and under are free). Tours leave Tuesday through Sunday at 10am and 1:30pm and Monday at 1:30pm, except holidays. No reservations are necessary—just show up, donations in hand. Tickets may be purchased in advance.

Tours by Isabelle (☎ **504/391-3544**), conducts small groups on a three-hour city tour in a comfortable, air-conditioned minibus. The tour covers the French Quarter, the cemeteries, Bayou St. John, City Park and the Lakefront, the universities, St. Charles Avenue, the Garden District, and the Superdome. The fare is $30, and departure times are 9am and 1:30pm. You should call as far in advance as possible to book. For $35 you can join her afternoon Combo Tour, which adds Longue Vue Gardens to all of the above.

Stop by the ✪**Jean Lafitte National Park and Preserve's Folklife and Visitor Center** at 419 Decatur St. (☎ **504/589-2636**) for details of the excellent free walking tours on a variety of topics conducted by National Park Service rangers. The History of New

Swamp Tours

In addition to the tour providers listed below, Jean Lafitte and Gray Line both offer a swamp tour (see "Organized Tours"). On all of the following tours you're likely to see alligators, bald eagles, waterfowl, egrets, owls, herons, osprey, feral hogs, otter, beaver, frogs, turtles, minks, raccoons, black bear, deer, and nutria.

Lil' Cajun Swamp Tours, Rt. 1, Box 397-A, Hwy. 301, Crown Point, LA (☎ **800/725-3213** or 504/689-3213), offers a good tour of Lafitte's bayous. Captain Cyrus Blanchard, "a Cajun French-speaking gentleman," knows the bayous like the back of his hand—mostly because it's where he lives. The tour lasts two hours and will run you about $16 for adults, $14 for seniors, and $12 for children if you drive yourself to the boat launch. If you need transportation it will cost you $30 for adults, $15 for children ages 6 to 12. (Note that the boat used on the Lil' Cajun Swamp Tours is much larger than the boat used on many of the other tours—it seats up to 67 people.)

Honey Island Swamp Tours, 106 Holly Ridge Dr., Slidell, LA (☎ **504/641-1769** or 504/242-5877), will take you by boat into the interior of Honey Island Swamp's "most beautiful and pristine areas" to view wildlife with native, professional, naturalist guides. Tours are approximately two hours long. Prices are $20 for adults, $10 for children under 12. Hotel pick-ups in New Orleans are available for a fee, or you can drive to the launch site yourself.

Gator Swamp Tours, also based in Slidell, LA (☎ **800/875-4287** or 504/484-6100), claims to offer the "longest and most personal swamp tour in the New Orleans area." Gator Swamp Tours takes visitors on a ride through Honey Island Swamp, beyond the bounds of the average swamp tour, into "the wilderness." Prices are $20 for adults, $10 for children under 12. Gator Swamp Tours now also offers a short nature walk in addition to boat tours. Like the other tour groups, Gator Swamp Tours offers hotel pick-ups for a fee.

Orleans tour covers about a mile in the French Quarter and brings to life New Orleans's history and the ethnic roots of the city's unique cultural mix. No reservations are required for this tour or the Tour du Jour (also in the Quarter), which is a "ranger's choice" that varies from day to day. You must book, however, for the Faubourg Promenade Tour which takes you for a walk in the Garden District. This tour is popular, so book a couple of days ahead.

✪ **Magic Walking Tours** (☎ 504/593-9693) at 1015 Iberville St. offers several guided walking tours daily. You might take a tour of St. Louis Cemetery No. 1, the French Quarter, or the Garden District. Or, if you're feeling a little more adventurous, try the Voodoo Tour or the Haunted House, Vampire, and Ghost-Hunt Walking Tour. The tour guides are excellent—not only do they enjoy their jobs, but they are extremely well educated about the city. Reservations are not necessary, but you should call ahead for tour schedules. Meeting places vary according to the tour you choose. Tours cost between $9 and $13 for adults and all children tour free.

"Roots" of New Orleans, A Heritage City Tour, 1750 St. Charles Ave., no. 202 (☎ 800/229-1872 or 504/522-7414), offers two black heritage tours daily from Thursday through Saturday. (At press time there were plans to offer the tours six days a week, so call ahead to see if the schedule has changed.) Experienced tour guides take visitors to some of Marie Laveau's favorite haunts, through the French Quarter, to the cemeteries, to the very roots of New Orleans jazz, and more. Rates are $27 for adults and $23 for children.

Gray Line, 2 Canal St., Suite 1300 (☎ 800/535-7786 or 504/587-0861), has tours of the entire city, including the French Quarter, in comfortable motor coaches. But take my word for it: The Quarter will demand a more in-depth examination than a view from a bus window. Take one of their excellent (and very informative) tours only after you've explored the Quarter in detail or as a prelude to doing so.

Boat Tours   The steamboat *Natchez,* 1340 World Trade Center of New Orleans (☎ 800/233-BOAT or 504/586-8777), a marvelous three-deck sternwheeler docked at the wharf behind the Jackson Brewery, offers two two-hour daytime cruises daily. The narration is by professional guides, and there are cocktail bars, an optional Creole buffet, and a gift shop aboard. The fares are $14.75 for adults ($18.75 in the evening not including dinner) and $7.25 for children ($10.75 in the evening not including dinner). Those under three ride free. Call for sailing schedule. Also, there is a jazz dinner cruise every evening. The buffet is optional. Call for the schedules and the prices.

The sternwheeler *John James Audubon,* 1300 World Trade Center of New Orleans (☎ 800/233-BOAT or 504/586-8777), offers an Aquarium-Zoo Cruise. Passengers travel the Mississippi by sternwheeler, tour the busy port, and dock to visit both the Audubon Zoo and the Aquarium of the Americas. There are four trips daily. Tours depart from the Riverwalk in front of the Aquarium at 10am, noon, 2pm, and 4pm. Return trips from the zoo are scheduled at 11am, 1pm, 3pm, and 5pm. Tickets for one-way or return trips can be purchased with or without aquarium and zoo admission. There is a combination ticket available that will save you several dollars. Call for prices, exact sailing schedule, and to make reservations.

The paddle-wheeler *Creole Queen,* 27 Poydras St. Wharf (☎ **800/445-4109** or 504/524-0814), departs from the Poydras Street Wharf adjacent to Riverwalk at 10:30am and 2pm for three-hour narrated excursions to the port and to the historic site of the Battle of New Orleans. There is also a 7pm jazz dinner cruise. The ship has a covered promenade deck, and its inner lounges are air-conditioned and heated. Buffet and cocktail services are available on all cruises. The fares are $14 for the daytime cruises and $39 for the nighttime jazz cruise (children $7 daytime, $18 nighttime; children under three are free). Call to confirm sailing schedules and current fares.

Carriage Tours   If you have even one romantic bone in your body, you'll find it hard to resist the authentic old horse-drawn (most are actually mule drawn, but who cares?) carriages that pick up passengers at Jackson Square. Each horse is decked out with ribbons, flowers, or even a hat, and each driver is apparently in fierce competition with all other drivers to win a "most unique city story" award. No matter which one you choose, you'll get a knowledgeable, nonstop monologue on historic buildings, fascinating events of the past, and a legend or two during the 2^1/$_4$-mile drive through the French Quarter. They're at the Decatur Street end of Jackson Square from 9am to midnight in good weather; the charge is $8 per adult and $5 for children under 12. *Note:* The carriage ride described here is *not* the one that will take you on your own private tour—private horse-carriage tours offered by **Good Old Days Buggies** (☎ **504/523-0804**), which include hotel or restaurant pick-up, will cost you significantly more.

Plantation Tours   A seven-hour River Road plantations tour is offered by **Gray Line,** 2345 New Orleans World Trade Center (☎ **504/587-0861**). The two plantations visited are Nottoway and Oak Alley. All admissions are included in the $50 charge. Tours, departing at 9am on Tuesday, Thursday, and Sunday, pick you up at and deliver you to your hotel. The cost of lunch at a country restaurant, however, is not included and generally runs $8 to $10, sometimes more.

If you prefer a smaller tour group, **Tours by Isabelle** (☎ **504/ 391-3544**) takes no more than 13 people in a comfortable minibus on an eight-hour expedition to visit Oak Alley, Madewood, and Nottoway plantations. Lunch in the elegant dining room of the Madewood Plantation mansion is included on this tour. The tour departs only when six or more people request it, so you might have to wait a day or two until they can get a large enough group together. Other tours offered by Tours by Isabelle include a 4¹/₂-hour Cajun Bayou Tour (the boat tour is 1¹/₂ hours); the five-hour Eastbank Plantation Tour (which includes a guided tours of Tezcuco Plantation with stops in front of Houmas House, Bocage, and Hermitage plantations); and the Grand Tour (a visit to Oak Alley Plantation, lunch, a Cajun Bayou Tour, and a stop in front of Destrehan plantation).

Antiques Tours   Antiquing in New Orleans can be a completely overwhelming experience, especially if you've never been to the city before. There are so many shops in the French Quarter and on Magazine Street that it's almost impossible to find what you're looking for without a little help. That's why Macon Riddle founded **Let's Go Antiquing!,** 1412 Fourth St. (☎ **504/899-3027**), in the mid-1980s. She'll organize and customize antique shopping tours to fit your needs. Hotel pick-up is standard on her tours, and if you're interested, she'll even make your lunch reservations for you. If you find something and you want it shipped home, she'll even take care of that. There's no doubt in my mind, Macon Riddle is the best in the business.

7

Shopping

*A*lmost anything you could want is for sale in New Orleans. And if you can't find what you're looking for, you can find someone to make it for you: The place is loaded with craftspeople and artisans who use such disparate materials as cast iron, wood, leather, fabric, brass, plastic, and precious metals.

Antique shops are really special here, many with patios and gardens that actually seem to enhance their goods. Some are located in old French Quarter homes, giving another dimension to browsing. And the emphasis that was always placed on fine home furnishings in New Orleans has left some of the loveliest antiques I've ever viewed. Many came from Europe in the early days; others were crafted right in the city by cabinetmakers, internationally known for their exquisite pieces. The **Royal Street Guild** (☎ **504/949-2222**), an association of some of the city's antique dealers, has put together brochures that are available at most hotels.

1 The Shopping Scene

Canal Place At the foot of Canal Street (365 Canal St.) where it reaches the Mississippi River, this stunning shopping center holds more than 50 shops, many of which are branches of some of this country's most elegant retailers. The three-tiered mall has polished marble floors, a landscaped atrium, fountains, and pools. Stores in this sophisticated setting include Brooks Brothers, Jaeger, Bally of Switzerland, Saks Fifth Avenue, and Laura Ashley. Open Monday to Wednesday and Friday to Saturday from 10am to 6pm; Thursday from 10am to 8pm; and Sunday from noon to 6pm.

The Esplanade The Esplanade, 1401 West Esplanade, houses more than 150 stores and specialty shops. Big-name stores that are represented include Macy's, Dillard's, Mervyn's, Yvonne LaFleur, and The Limited. There is also a large food court. Open Monday to Saturday from 10am to 9pm, and Sunday from noon to 6pm.

The French Market Shops within the Market begin on Decatur Street across from Jackson Square, and include candy, cookware, fashions, crafts, toys, New Orleans memorabilia, and candles. Open from 10am to 6pm (Farmer's Market Café du Monde open 24 hours).

Jackson Brewery   Just across from Jackson Square at 600–620 Decatur St., the old brewery building has been transformed into a joyful jumble of shops, cafes, delicatessens, restaurants, and entertainment. The 125 shops and eateries within its walls include fashions, gourmet and Cajun-Creole foodstuffs, toys, hats, crafts, pipes, posters, and souvenirs. The latest addition to this mall is a branch of the theme restaurant Planet Hollywood. Keep in mind that many shops in the Brewery close at 5:30 or 6pm, before the Brewery itself closes. Open Sunday to Thursday from 10am to 10pm, and Friday to Saturday from 10am to 9pm.

Julia Street   From Camp Street over toward the river on Julia Street, you'll find great contemporary art galleries lining the street. Of course, some of the works are a bit pricey, but there's a lot that's absolutely affordable if you're interested in collecting. You'll find many of them listed below.

Magazine Street   This major uptown thoroughfare runs from Canal Street to Audubon Park, with some 6 miles of more than 140 shops (some of which are listed below), some in 19th-century brick storefronts, others in quaint, cottagelike buildings. Among the offerings are antiques, art galleries, boutiques, crafts, and dolls.

New Orleans Centre   New Orleans's newest shopping center, New Orleans Centre at 1400 Poydras features a glass atrium and includes upscale shops like Lord & Taylor and Macy's. There are three levels of specialty shops and restaurants. Open Monday to Saturday from 10am to 8pm and Sunday from noon to 6pm.

Riverbend   The Riverbend district is in the Carrollton area. To reach it, ride the St. Charles Avenue streetcar to stop 44, then walk down Maple Street one block to Dublin Park, the site of an old public market once lined with open stalls. Nowadays, renovated shops inhabit the old general store, a produce warehouse made of bargeboard, and the town surveyor's raised-cottage home. Among the outstanding shops are Yvonne LaFleur, whose romantic fashions have appeared on TV and movie screens; and the Cache Pot, with a concentration of unusual, high-quality gifts.

Riverwalk   This popular shopping development at 1 Poydras St. is an exciting covered mall that runs right along the river from Poydras Street to the Convention Center. Among the 140 specialty shops at this location, you'll find Eddie Bauer, The Limited, The Sharper Image, and Banana Republic, plus several eateries and periodic free entertainment. Open Monday to Thursday from 10am to 9pm, Friday and Saturday from 10am to 10pm, and Sunday from 12:30pm to 5:30pm.

2   Shopping A to Z

ANTIQUES

Audubon Antiques. 2025 Magazine St. ☎ **504/581-5704.** Mon–Sat 10am–5pm; Sun noon–5pm.

Audubon has everything from collectible curios to authentic antique treasures at reasonable prices.

DoAurat Antiques. 3009 Magazine St. ☎ **504/897-3210** or 800/676-8640. Mon and Wed–Sat 10am–5pm.

Owners Robert and Martha Lady collect and import incredibly beautiful Indo-Portuguese and Anglo-Indian colonial furniture as well as Oriental rugs, dhurries, kilims, and other collectibles.

Boyer Antiques—Dolls & Buttons. 241 and 328 Chartres St. ☎ **504/522-4513.** Daily 9:30am–5pm.

In addition to an assortment of antiques, you'll find an enchanting collection of old dolls and doll furniture.

Charbonnet & Charbonnet, Inc. 2929 Magazine St. ☎ **504/891-9948.** Mon–Sat 9am–5pm.

If country pine is what you're looking for, you'll find it at Charbonnet and Charbonnet. They have some beautiful English and Irish pieces. In addition, custom furnishings are made on-site.

French Antique Shop. 225 Royal St. ☎ **504/524-9861.** Mon–Fri 9am–5pm; Sat 10am–3pm.

This shop specializes in 18th- and 19th-century French furnishings, mirrors, statues, lighting fixtures, and marble fireplace mantels. Other items include Oriental porcelains and collectibles.

Kiel's Antiques. 325 Royal St. ☎ **504/522-4552.** Mon–Sat 9am–5pm.

This lovely antique shop has a fine collection of French and English antiques, as well as decorative items.

Le Wicker Gazebo. 3436 Magazine St. ☎ **504/899-1355.** Daily 10am–4pm.

New and antique wicker furnishings, including miniature versions for children.

✪ **Lucullus.** 610 Chartres St. ☎ **504/528-9620.** Mon–Sat 9am–5pm.

An unusual shop, Lucullus has a wonderful collection of culinary antiques as well as 17th-, 18th-, and 19th-century furnishings to "complement the grand pursuits of cooking, dining, and imbibing."

Magazine Arcade Antiques. 3017 Magazine St. ☎ **504/895-5451.** Mon–Sat 10am–5pm.

This large and fascinating shop once housed the Garden District's classiest mercantile. Today it holds an exceptional collection of 18th- and 19th-century European, Asian, and American furnishings; music boxes; dollhouse miniatures; European and Oriental porcelain; cloisonné and lacquer; cameos; opera glasses; old medical equipment; wind-up phonographs; antique toys; and scores of other items. Try to plan plenty of time to browse through it all.

Manheim Galleries. 403–409 Royal St. ☎ **504/568-1901.** Mon–Sat 9am–5pm.

At Manheim Galleries you'll find an enormous collection of Continental, English, and Oriental furnishings. There is also a collection of porcelains, jade, silver, and fine painting. Manheim Galleries is also the agent for Boehm Birds.

Miss Edna's Antiques. 2029 Magazine St. ☎ **504/524-1897.** Call for hours.

Miss Edna's has a wonderful selection of furniture, specialty items, and curios.

✪ **Rothschild's Antiques.** 241 and 321 Royal St. ☎ **504/523-5816** or 504/523-2281. Mon–Sat 9am–5pm.

Some of the most interesting things you'll find here are antique and custom-made jewelry pieces. There's also a fine selection of antique silver, marble mantels, porcelains, and English and French furnishings.

Royal Antiques. 307–309 Royal St. ☎ **504/524-7033.** Mon–Sat 9:15am–5:30pm.

Royal specializes in 18th- and 19th-century French and English furnishings as well as chandeliers and brass and copper accessories. There's another location at 715 Bienville St.

Sigle's Antiques & Metalcraft. 935 Royal St. ☎ **504/522-7647.** Mon–Fri 10am–4pm.

If you've fallen in love with the lacy ironwork that drips from French Quarter balconies, this is the place to pick out some pieces to take home. In addition, Sigle's has converted some of the ironwork into useful household items, such as plant holders.

Whisnant Galleries. 222 Chartres St. ☎ **504/524-9766.** Mon–Sat 9:30am–5:30pm.

The quantity and variety of merchandise in this shop is mind-boggling. You'll find all sorts of unusual and unique collectibles, including items from Morocco, Ethiopia, Russia, Greece, South America, North Africa, and the Middle East.

ART GALLERIES

In addition to those listed below, there are a great number of galleries in what used to be the warehouse district and is now a center for the arts. You can pick up a brochure called "Arts in the Warehouse District" that lists a fairly large number of galleries on Julia Street and some of the surrounding streets. Though there are many wonderful galleries on Royal Street, don't forget the old warehouse district, especially if you're interested in contemporary art.

American Indian Art. 824 Chartres St. ☎ **504/586-0479.** Mon and Wed–Fri 10am–5pm; Sat 10am–6pm; and Sun noon–5pm.

If you're a collector of Native American arts and crafts, this is the place for you. American Indian Art carries a wide variety of antique and modern Native American baskets, jewelry, sculpture, beadwork (Plains and Woodlands), kachinas, pottery, and weavings. Louisiana tribes represented include Koasati and Chitimacha. The work of the Zuni, Navajo, and Hopi Indians is also shown here.

Ariodante. 535 Julia St. ☎ **504/524-3233.** Mon–Sat 11am–5pm. Closed Mon during daylight saving time.

A contemporary craft gallery, Ariodante features hand-crafted furniture, glass, ceramics, jewelry, and decorative accessories by nationally acclaimed artists. Rotating shows offer a detailed look at works by various artists.

Arius Art Tiles. 504 St. Peter St. ☎ **504/529-1665.** Daily 9:30am–5:30pm.

If you've been to Santa Fe you might recognize some of the art tiles that are being sold here—many of the tiles are made in Santa Fe, and Arius has a sister gallery in New Mexico. Southwest as well as Louisiana designs are available. Custom orders are taken.

Bergen Galleries. 730 Royal St. ☎ **504/523-7882** or 800/621-6179. Daily 9am–9pm.

Bergen Galleries has the city's largest selection of posters and limited-edition graphics—including New Orleans works; Mardi Gras; jazz; and artists such as Erté, Icart, Nagel, Maimon, Tarkay, as well as a large collection of works by sought-after African American artists. The service from Margarita and her staff is friendly and extremely personable.

Bryant Galleries. 524 Royal St. ☎ **504/525-5584.** Sun–Wed 10am–5:30pm; Thurs–Fri 10am–8pm; Sat 10am–10pm.

This gallery represents renowned artists Ed Dwight, Fritzner Lamour, and Leonardo Nierman. Contemporary art is what you'll find here, including jazz bronzes, glasswork, and graphics.

☉ Casey Willems Pottery. 3919 Magazine St. ☎ **504/899-1174.** Mon–Sat 10am–5pm.

Watch Casey Willems create functional art pottery before your very eyes as you browse his gallery. You'll find the usual vases and teapots, but Willems has been known to create some uniquely functional items as well.

Circle Gallery. 316 Royal St. ☎ **504/523-1350.** Mon–Sat 10am–6pm; Sun 11am–6pm.

This gallery features contemporary sculpture, graphics, and paintings by internationally known artists like Yaacov Agam, Victor Vasarely, Sandro Cia, Rene Gruau, Yvari, and Erte.

☉ The Davis Galleries. 3964 Magazine St. ☎ **504/897-0780.** Tues–Sat 10am–5pm.

The Davis Galleries features Central and West African traditional art. Works on display might include sculpture, costuming, basketry, textiles, weapons, and jewelry.

Dixon & Dixon of Royal. 237 and 318 Royal St. ☎ **504/524-0282** or 800/848-5148. Mon–Sat 9am–5:30pm; Sun 10am–5pm.

Dixon and Dixon features 18th- and 19th-century European fine art, antiques, jewelry, clocks, and Oriental rugs.

Dyansen Gallery. 433 Royal St. ☎ **504/523-2902.** Mon–Thurs and Sun 10am–6pm; Fri–Sat 10am–9pm.

A branch of the Dyansen family galleries (there are others in San Francisco and New York), this gallery features graphics, sculpture, and original gouaches by Erté. Other artists represented include Leroy Neiman, Richard Estes, and Paul Wegner.

Endangered Species. 619 Royal St. ☎ **504/568-9855.** Mon–Sat 10am–5pm; Sun 11am–4pm.

The owners of Endangered Species have traveled the world (35 countries) collecting art objects and artifacts. Here you'll find tribal masks, unusual jewelry, carved ivories, and hand-woven textiles.

Galerie Royale, Ltd. 312 Royal St. ☎ **504/523-1588.** Daily 10am–6pm (open at 11am on some Sundays).

If you appreciate the works of William Tolliver (whether you just want to browse or buy), you'll find his museum-quality work here, as well as some work by Chagall, Dali, and Miró.

Galerie Simonne Stern. 518 Julia St. ☎ **504/529-1118.** Tues–Fri 10am–6pm.

Galerie Simonne Stern features paintings, drawings, and sculptures by contemporary artists. Recent shows included the works of Sam Gilliam, George Dunbar, Richard Johnson, James McGarrell, Lynda Benglis, Albert Paley, and Arthur Silverman.

A Gallery for Fine Photography. 322 Royal St. ☎ **504/568-1313.** Daily 10am–6pm.

A Gallery for Fine Photography specializes in 19th- and 20th-century rare photographs and books, and regular exhibits include the works of Ansel Adams, Alfred Stieglitz, and Edward Curtis. Recent exhibits included Walker Evans, Berenice Abbott, Helmut Newton, O. Winston Link, and Diane Arbus.

Hanson Gallery. 229 Royal St. ☎ **504/524-8211.** Mon–Sat 10am–6pm; Sun 11am–5pm.

Hanson Galleries shows paintings, sculpture, and limited-edition prints of contemporary artists such as Peter Max, Frederick Hart, Pradzynski, Anoro, Thysell, Deckbar, Zjawinska, Erickson, Leroy Neiman, Richard MacDonald, and Behrens.

Hilderbrand Gallery. 4524 Magazine St. ☎ **504/895-3312.** Daily 10am–9pm.

Hilderbrand Galleries features contemporary works of fine art in all mediums by international, national, and local artists, including the works of Ding Massimo Boccuni, Walter Rutkowski, Christian Stock, Robert Rucker, Robert Griffeth, Cort Savage, Lynda Freese, Mark Westervelt, Janet Glodner, and Karl Heinz-Strohle.

Importicos. 736 Royal St. ☎ **504/523-3100.** Daily 10am–6pm.

If you're interested in hand-crafted imports from Central America and Indonesia, stop by Importicos, where you'll find a selection of hand-crafted silver jewelry, pottery, textiles, antique and museum reproduction earrings, and leather, wood, stone, and metal items. There's another store at 517 St. Louis St. (☎ **504/523-0306**).

Kurt E. Schon, Ltd. 523 Royal St. ☎ **504/524-5462.** Mon–Sat 9am–5pm.

Here you'll find this country's largest inventory of 19th-century European paintings. Works include French and British Impressionist and post-Impressionist paintings as well as art from the Royal Academy and The French Salon. Only a fraction of the paintings in the gallery's inventory are housed at this location, but if you're a serious collector you can make an appointment to visit the St. Louis Street gallery.

Nahan Galleries. 540 Royal St. ☎ **504/524-8696.** Mon–Sat 9:30am–6pm; Sun 11am–6pm.

Nahan specializes in works of major contemporary artists and publishes graphics for Tobiasse, Papart, Coignard, Olbinski, and others.

✪ **New Orleans School of Glassworks.** 727 Magazine St. ☎ **504/529-7277.** Mon–Sat 11am–5pm.

This place is difficult to categorize, simply because it serves multiple purposes—allowing artists and blossoming artists in the area of glasswork to give and take classes. Accomplished glass artists and master printmakers who teach at the school are allowed to show and sell their pieces here in the gallery. Absolutely unique to the area, it is worth a visit during gallery hours. Here, within 20,000 square feet of studio space, are a 550-pound, hot molten tank of glass and a pre–Civil War press. Daily glassblowing, fusing, and slumping demonstrations are offered. Classes in glassblowing, kiln-fired glass, hand-engraved printmaking, papermaking, and bookbinding are offered.

The Rodrigue Gallery of New Orleans. 721 Royal St. ☎ **504/581-4244.** Daily 10am–6pm.

If you're visiting New Orleans there's no way you'll miss Cajun artist George Rodrigue's "Blue Dog," even if you want to. Rodrigue began painting portraits of his dog (a terrier-mix that had already died) for a children's book in 1984, and he hasn't stopped since. His work is known internationally and he is represented in galleries in Munich as well as Yokohama. You will either be instantly charmed by the dog's image (as millions are) or you'll quickly grow weary of seeing its likeness all around the city.

Shadyside Pottery. 3823 Magazine St. ☎ **504/897-1710.** Mon–Sat 10am–5pm.

If you want to see another master potter at work, Shadyside Pottery is an excellent place to stop. Charles Bohn, who apprenticed in

Japan, can be seen at his wheel all day on weekdays and until midafternoon on Saturday. In addition to Bohn's own work, he carries a selection of Japanese kites (by Mitsuyoshi Kawamoto) as well as some glass work.

Trade Folk Art Import Export. 828 Chartres St. ☎ **504/596-6827.** Daily 10am–5pm.

Taina and Kelly travel to Mexico frequently and bring back some wonderful pieces of folk art. If you know nothing about Mexican folk art, you really should stop by and look around. Trade Folk Art also features southern folk artists. They'll also give you an education if you ask.

BOOKS

The **Maple Street Bookshop,** 7523 Maple St. (☎ **504/866-4916**), has three locations, including the **Maple Street Children's Book Shop,** next door at 7529 Maple St. (☎ **504/861-2105**); and **Maple Street's Old Metarie Book Shop,** in Old Metairie Village, 701 Metairie Rd. (☎ **504/832-8937**). There's also **De Ville Books and Prints,** 1 Shell Square (☎ **504/525-1846**); and **Beaucoup Books,** 5415 Magazine St. (☎ **504/895-2663**). **Little Professor Book Center of New Orleans,** 1000 S. Carrollton Ave. (☎ **504/866-7646**), stocks one of the best general collections.

Beckham's Bookshop. 228 Decatur St. ☎ **504/522-9875.** Daily 10am–6pm.

Beckham's has two entire floors of old editions and some rare secondhand books that will tie up your whole afternoon or morning if you don't tear yourself away. The owners also operate Librairie Bookshop, 823 Chartres St., which you'll surely have found if you're a book lover. Beckham's also has thousands of classical LPs.

Bookstar. 414 N. Peters St. ☎ **504/523-6411.** Daily 10am–midnight.

Bookstar is a large, attractive chain bookstore in the Jackson Brewery complex. Without doubt, it stocks one of the largest selections of books and magazines in the city, and its enthusiastic and knowledgeable staff can help you find the printed word on virtually any subject you can name.

✪ **Faulkner House Books.** 624 Pirates Alley. ☎ **504/524-2940.** Daily 10am–6pm.

This is a small bookstore with a big history. It was here that southern fiction writer and Nobel Prize winner William Faulkner lived while he was writing *Soldiers' Pay.* Today the shop holds a large collection of first-edition Faulkners, including copies of *The Sound and the Fury,* as well as rare and first-edition classics by many other authors. For book lovers, this shop is a must stop on a trip to New Orleans.

George Herget Books. 3109 Magazine St. ☎ **504/891-5595.** Mon–Sat 10am–5:30pm.

George Herget Books is another of New Orleans's great bookstores. More than 20,000 rare and used books covering absolutely every subject imaginable are available for your browsing and collecting pleasure.

Old Children's Books. 734 Royal St. ☎ **504/525-3655.** Mon–Sat 10am–1pm.

Just as its name indicates, Old Children's Books carries thousands of antique and rare children's books from the 19th century through the 1970s. Ring the buzzer to gain entrance to the shop. The courtyard alone is worth the visit.

Olive Tree Book Store. 927 Royal St. ☎ **504/523-8041.** Daily 10am–10pm.

I love this bookstore because it is absolutely piled high, wall to wall, with books—there's hardly room to walk around. They carry old and rare books, as well as records and magazines.

CANDIES & PRALINES

Aunt Sally's Praline Shops. 810 Decatur St. ☎ **504/524-5107.** Daily 8am–8pm.

At Aunt Sally's, in the French Market, you can watch skilled workers perform the 150-year-old process of cooking the original Creole pecan pralines right before your eyes. You'll know they're fresh. The large store also has a broad selection of regional cookbooks, books on the history of New Orleans and its environs, Creole and Cajun foods, folk and souvenir dolls, and local memorabilia. In addition, Aunt Sally's has a collection of zydeco, Cajun, rhythm and blues, and jazz CDs and cassettes. They'll ship any of your purchases, which can considerably lighten the load going home.

✪ **Leah's Candy Kitchen.** 714 St. Louis St. ☎ **504/523-5662.** Mon–Sat 10am–10pm.

Leah's, in my opinion, has the best pralines in the city. (You might prefer one of the others, though—I suggest you torture yourself and try them all.) Everything, from the candy fillings to the incredible chocolate-covered pecan brittle, is made from scratch.

COSTUMES & MASKS

A number of shops specialize in Mardi Gras finery. And remember, New Orleanians often sell their costumes after Ash Wednesday, and you can sometimes pick up a one-time-worn outfit at a small fraction of its cost new.

✪ **Little Shop of Fantasy.** 523 Dumaine St. ☎ **504/529-4243.** Mon–Tues and Thurs–Sat 10am–6pm; Sun 1–6pm.

In the Little Shop of Fantasy, owners Mike Stark, Laura and Anne Guccione, and Jill Kellys host a number of local artists and more than 20 mask makers. Mike creates the feathered masks, Jill does the velvet hats and costumes, and Laura and Anne make homemade toiletries. Some of the masks and hats are just fun and fanciful, but there are some extraordinary and beautiful ones as well.

Mardi Gras Center. 831 Chartres St. ☎ **504/524-4384.** Mon–Sat 10am–5pm.

Mardi Gras Center carries sizes 2 to 50 and has a wide selection of new, ready-made costumes as well as used outfits. It also carries all accessories such as beads, doubloons, wigs, masks, hats, makeup, jewelry, and Mardi Gras decorations. Mardi Gras Center is also a good place to stop for Halloween supplies.

FOOD

Café du Monde Coffee Shop. 800 Decatur St. ☎ **504/581-2914.** Daily 24 hours.

If you want to try your hand at making those scrumptious beignets, you can buy the mix at the Café du Monde, in the French Market. To make it complete, pick up a can of their famous coffee, a special blend of coffee and chicory. The shop also has a very good mail-order service (☎ **800/772-2927;** fax 504/587-0847).

Creole Delicacies Gourmet Shop. 533 St. Ann St. ☎ **504/523-6425.** Mon–Thurs 9:30am–9pm; Fri–Sat 9:30am–10pm; Sun 10am–6pm.

Cajun and Creole packaged foods and mixes are what you'll find here. Fill your shopping basket with everything from jambalaya and gumbo mix to rémoulade and hot sauces. Creole Delicacies is also located at Riverwalk Marketplace.

Louisiana Potpourri. Canal Place Shopping Center, 333 Canal St. No. 202. ☎ **504/524-9023.** Mon–Wed and Fri–Sat 10am–6pm; Thurs 10am–8pm; and Sun noon–6pm.

If you want to take home a potpourri of New Orleans flavors, this is a great place to begin shopping. They have everything from gumbo flavoring to Cajun hot nuts (one of my favorites). Gift baskets are available, and Louisiana Potpourri will ship things home for you.

Orleans Coffee Exchange. 712 Orleans Ave. ☎ **504/522-5710.** Mon–Fri 8am–6pm; Sat 9am–6pm; Sun 10am–6pm.

Java junkies won't be able to leave New Orleans without a visit to the Orleans Coffee Exchange. The 500 varieties of coffee beans here come from all over the world. There are also more than 350 flavored coffees as well as scores of exotic teas.

HATS

In addition to the shops listed below, you can also get fun costume hats at Little Shop of Fantasy, listed above.

Meyer the Hatter. 120 St. Charles Ave. ☎ **504/525-1048** or 800/882-4287. Mon–Sat 9:45am–5:45pm.

Meyer's has one of the largest selections of fine hats and caps in the South. Men will find distinguished head wear with labels such as Stetson, Dobbs, and Borsalino in this fine shop, which opened in 1894 and is now run by third-generation members of the same family.

Rine Chapeaux. Riverwalk No. 1 Poydras St. ☎ **504/523-7463.** Mon–Thurs 10am–9pm; Fri–Sat 10am–10pm; Sun 10am–7pm.

Here you'll find more than 300 different styles of hats and caps for men and women. Women will also enjoy browsing through the sizable collection of hair accessories.

MUSIC

Beckham's Bookshop. 228 Decatur St. ☎ **504/522-9875.** Daily 10am–6pm.

It's better known for its fine collection of used books (see above), but Beckham's also has a large selection of second-hand classical music records.

Louisiana Music Factory. 225 N. Peters. ☎ **504/523-1094.** Daily 10am–7pm.

This popular music store carries a large selection of regional tunes, including Cajun, zydeco, R&B, jazz, blues, and gospel. There's also a collection of books, posters, and T-shirts.

Record Ron's. 1129 Decatur St. ☎ **504/561-9444.** Daily 11am–7pm.

Record Ron's has a good selection of classic rock LPs, as well as jazz, Cajun, zydeco, R&B, and blues. At Record Ron's you'll find thousands of 45s, CDs, and cassettes. There's also a large collection of T-shirts, posters, sheet music, rubber stamps, music memorabilia, and jewelry. Record Ron's Stuff, another store, is located at 239 Chartres Street (☎ **504/522-2239**).

THE OCCULT

The Bottom of the Cup Tearoom. 732 Royal St. ☎ **504/523-1204.** Mon–Sat 9am–9pm; Sun 11am–7pm.

At the Bottom of the Cup Tearoom, psychics and clairvoyants specialize in palm reading, crystal gazing, tea-leaf reading, and tarot. You can also get your astrological chart done. It's been open since 1929 and bills itself as the "oldest tearoom in the United States." In addition to having a psychic consultation you can also purchase books, jewelry, crystal balls, tarot cards, crystals, and healing wands here.

Marie Laveau's House of Voodoo. 739 Bourbon St. ☎ **504/581-3751.** Sun–Thurs 10am–11:30pm; Fri–Sat 10am–12:30 or 1:30am.

Marie Laveau's House of Voodoo is the perfect place to stop if you're looking for some "touristy" voodoo items to take home to friends. You'll find all sorts of mojos and voodoo dolls here. In addition, there's an on-site psychic and palm reader.

PUPPETS

Pontalba Historical Puppetorium. 514 St. Peter St. ☎ **504/522-0344** or 504/944-8144. Daily 9:30am–5:30pm.

There's an excellent puppet presentation of New Orleans history here in Jackson Square, but you can also purchase puppets. In fact, the puppetorium has the largest collection in the United States.

TOYS

Le Petit Soldier Shop. 528 Royal St. ☎ **504/523-7741.** Mon–Sat 10am–4pm.

Local artists create the two-inch-high masterpieces in this shop. The miniatures depict soldiers from ancient Greece up to Desert Storm, and many of the miniatures actually resemble major figures in military history, like Eisenhower, Grant, Lee, Hitler, and Napoleon. There's a large collection of medals and decorations.

The Little Toy Shoppe. 900 Decatur St. ☎ **504/522-6588.** Daily 9am–8pm. Closed Christmas, Mardi Gras, Thanksgiving, and Easter.

The dolls here are some of the most beautiful I've ever seen, especially the Madame Alexander and Effanbee ones, and the New Orleans–made bisque and rag dolls. In addition to "heroes" wood toys from Germany and "All God's Children" collectibles, there are cuddly stuffed animals, tea sets, toy soldiers, and miniature cars and trucks.

UMBRELLAS

The Umbrella Lady. 1107 Decatur St. ☎ **504/523-7791.** Hours vary, so call ahead.

They call her "The Umbrella Lady," but her real name is Anne B. Lane. You'll find her in her upstairs studio. A Quarter fixture, she's the creator of wonderful Secondline umbrellas as well as fanciful "southern belle" parasols. Look for the umbrellas displayed on her balcony.

WOODCRAFTS

Idea Factory. 838 Chartres St. ☎ **504/524-5195** or 800/524-IDEA. Mon–Sat 10am–6pm; Sun noon–5pm.

One of my favorite shops in the French Quarter, the Idea Factory features all sorts of hand-crafted wood items, including toys, kinetic sculptures, door harps, signs, boxes, and office supplies (business-card holders, in/out trays, etc.). Many of the items are made right on the premises so if you're lucky you might get to see one of the craftspeople at work. Also featured is the jewelry of Thomas Mann.

8

New Orleans After Dark

*J*azz, Hurricanes, Pat O'Brien's, strippers, and cross-dressers: the French Quarter, in all its glory. New Orleans earned its Bacchanalian reputation and still deserves it—it's the only city in the country where it's legal to drink alcohol in the streets. The French Quarter seems to remove inhibitions as quickly as a triple bourbon: Anything goes here, and often does until sunrise. (New Orleans has no closure laws, so some bars and clubs stay open throughout the night, particularly during Carnival.)

Jazz was born here in Storyville cathouses, and while the brothels are gone, the music still lingers. At the moment when Buddy Bolden blew the first notes of jazz from his cornet near the end of the last century, New Orleans guaranteed its reputation as a music city. In years to come jazz greats such as Louis Armstrong, Jelly Roll Morton, and later Harry Connick, Jr., and the Marsalises were to hone their skills in French Quarter clubs. In the past several decades, however, musicians such as the Neville brothers and Dr. John have broadened the focus of the music scene beyond its original jazz roots. Today, jazz and blues share the music marquee with Cajun, zydeco, R&B, world beat, rock, and pop.

That's not to imply, though, that jazz has abandoned the place of its birth. Performers both black and white, both newcomers and old-timers, join together to keep the traditional sound alive at all hours in the French Quarter and after dark outside the Quarter. You'll still find uninhibited dancers performing in the streets outside jazz spots (sometimes passing the hat to onlookers); jazz funerals for departed musicians (the trip to that final resting place accompanied by sorrowful dirges and "second liners" who shuffle and clap hands to a mournful beat); the return (a joyful, swinging celebration of the deceased's "liberation"); and occasionally a street parade (even when it isn't Carnival), complete with brass band.

The bars and clubs listed below are some of the hot spots at the time this edition was updated; however, the notoriously fickle fortunes of the nightclub business make it your best bet to walk up and down Bourbon Street and follow the sounds of your favorite type of music and the loudest (or quietest) crowd to a spot you might like to try. Most places open for happy hour, around noon in most cases, and stay open until the wee hours since New Orleans has no closure law.

Note: For safety reasons, it's best to take a cab to and from any and all of the nightspots outside the French Quarter.

For up-to-date information on what's happening around town when you're there, look for current editions of *Where, Gambit,* and Offbeat, all of which are free and are distributed in most hotels. You can also check out *Offbeat* magazine on the internet (http://www.nola.com). Once you get to the nola home page, go to the music and entertainment section, and you'll have no trouble finding the magazine there. Other sources would be the *Times-Picayune's* daily entertainment calendar as well as Friday's **La-gniappe** section of the newspaper. Additionally, **WWOZ** (90.7 FM) broadcasts the local music schedule several times throughout the day. If you miss the broadcasts, call **504/840-4040,** WWOZ's "Tower Records's Second Line," for the same information.

1 Jazz & Blues

This being New Orleans, jazz and blues are everywhere—you just have to look a little harder than you had to in the good old days. The clubs listed below feature jazz and/or blues on a nightly (or almost nightly) basis, but there are other places worth consideration that may only offer live music once or twice a week. **Court of Two Sisters** (see Chapter 5) has a great jazz brunch, as does **Cafe Sbisa,** 1011 Decatur St. (☎ **504/522-5565**), on Sundays. In addition, **Joe's Cozy Corner,** 1532 Ursulines (☎ **504/561-9216**), in the Treme section of New Orleans has live jazz on Sundays (not a great neighborhood though), and **Crescent City Brewhouse,** 527 Decatur St. (☎ **504/522-0571**), features modern jazz bands in the afternoons on Friday, Saturday, and Sunday. Many hotel lounges and bars also feature live jazz performances, so be sure to check with your concierge.

THE FRENCH QUARTER & THE FAUBOURG MARIGNY

Cosimo's Bar. 1201 Burgundy St. ☎ **504/561-8110.** $5–$10 cover.

If you're just wandering around in the heart of the French Quarter you're going to miss a great place for traditional jazz jams. Cosimo's is in the Quarter, but on the outer edges, so its still relatively safe,

French Quarter Nightlife

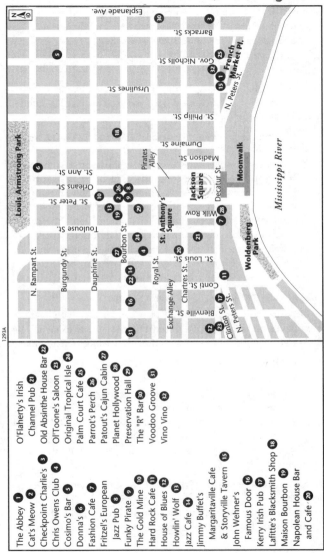

The Abbey **1**
Cat's Meow **2**
Checkpoint Charlie's **3**
Chris Owens Club **4**
Cosimo's **5**
Donna's **6**
Fashion Cafe **7**
Fritzel's European
Jazz Pub **8**
Funky Pirate **9**
The Gold Mine **10**
Hard Rock Cafe **11**
House of Blues **12**
Howlin' Wolf **13**
Jazz Cafe **14**
Jimmy Buffet's
Margaritaville Cafe
& Storyville Tavern **15**
John Wehner's
Famous Door **16**
Kerry Irish Pub **17**
Lafitte's Blacksmith Shop **18**
Maison Bourbon **19**
Napolean House Bar
and Cafe **20**

O'Flaherty's Irish
Channel Pub **21**
Old Absinthe House Bar **22**
Ol'Toone's Saloon **23**
Original Tropical Isle **24**
Palm Court Cafe **25**
Parrot's Perch **26**
Patout's Cajun Cabin **27**
Planet Hollywood **28**
Preservation Hall **29**
The "R" Bar **30**
Voodoo Groove **31**
Vino Vino **32**

1293A

143

but if you're walking try to go with someone and stay with the crowd if possible. Live music begins at 8pm on Wednesday, Friday, and Saturday and goes until about midnight.

Donna's. 800 N. Rampart St. ☎ **504/596-6914.** Cover varies according to performer.

Located right on the edge of the French Quarter, Donna's is known for showcasing talented local brass bands. This place is definitely worth a stop for serious music lovers.

Fritzel's European Jazz Pub. 733 Bourbon St. ☎ **504/561-0432.** No cover (one-drink minimum per set, per person).

You might walk right past this small establishment, but that would be a big mistake, for since 1973 this 1831 building has attracted some of the city's best musicians to play on its tiny stage in back. In addition to the regular weekend program of late-night jazz (Friday and Saturday from 10:30pm, Sunday from 10pm), there are frequent jam sessions here in the wee hours during the week, when musicians end their stints elsewhere and gather to play "Musicians' Music." The full bar also stocks a variety of Schnapps (served ice-cold) and German beers on tap and in bottles.

Funky Pirate. 727 Bourbon St. ☎ **504/523-1960.** $5 cover.

Decorated to resemble a pirates' "den," and packed with loud beer-drinking fraternity types, the Funky Pirate lives up to its name. "Big" Al Carson and the Blues Masters provide live blues entertainment.

House of Blues. 225 Decatur St. ☎ **504/529-2583.** Cover $5–$25.

Live blues performances are staged here in Dan Aykroyd's second House of Blues (the first was opened in Boston), which is one of the largest and most advanced venues of its genre. Recent musical performers included Bob Dylan, Eric Clapton, Bo Diddley, Fats Domino, and Taj Mahal among others. There's a gospel brunch offered every Sunday at 11am and 2pm (reservations are strongly recommended). Friday brings $1 beers and free snacks.

Jazz Cafe. 411 Bourbon St. ☎ **504/522-7623.** Cover varies according to performer.

For live jazz and R&B, the best time to visit the Jazz Cafe is in the afternoon. The sound and lighting here are excellent; there's a decent bar as well.

Jimmy Buffett's Margaritaville Cafe & Storyville Tavern. 1104 Decatur St. ☎ **504/592-2565** or 504/592-2552 (concert line). No cover.

Live entertainment is featured nightly at Jimmy Buffett's. Local musical stars Marva Wright and Charmaine Neville perform regularly, and nationally known blues acts are frequently scheduled as well; Jimmy himself is known to show up and play a set from time to time. Food is served daily from 11am to 10:30pm (midnight on Friday and Saturday).

John Wehner's Famous Door. 339 Bourbon St. ☎ **504/522-7626.** One-drink minimum per set.

Extant since 1934, the Famous Door is the oldest music club on Bourbon Street. There's jazz in the afternoon, and in the evening you're invited to dance to jazz and blues from the 1960s through the 1990s.

Maison Bourbon. 641 Bourbon St. ☎ **504/522-8818.** One-drink minimum.

You might start your evening at Maison Bourbon, which keeps its doors open to the sidewalk and employs three bands every day to play from 2:15 or 3:15pm to midnight or 2am. Big-time jazz players include Wallace Davenport, Steve Slocum, and Tommy Yetta.

Old Absinthe House Bar. 400 Bourbon St. ☎ **504/525-8108.** No cover.

Don't confuse this place with the Old Absinthe House at 240 Bourbon. That's right, they both have the same name, and what's more, they're both entitled to it. The one on the corner of Bourbon and Bienville streets (that's No. 240) can claim the original site, while all the original fixtures are now to be found at No. 400, on the corner of Bourbon and Conti. That situation came about when federal agents padlocked the original (it was operating as a speakeasy) during the 1920s, and some enterprising soul broke in, removed the bar, the register, 19th-century prints, ceiling fans, an antique French clock, and a handsome set of marble-based fountains once used to drip water into absinthe (which has been banned in the United States since 1918 because it's a narcotic). They all turned up soon afterward in the establishment on the corner a block away, and New Orleans was blessed with two "original" Old Absinthe Houses. Anyway, it's the one at 400 Bourbon where you'll find rhythm and blues and progressive jazz—and you'll find drinks only at the other. Beginning at 9pm nightly, the music is continuous, sometimes with as many as three groups alternating, until all hours. There's no legal shutdown time in New Orleans, and it isn't unusual to find things still going strong here as dawn breaks. On weekends there's also daytime music. Blues dominate on the bandstand. Drinks start at $2.

Palm Court Café. 1204 Decatur St. ☎ **504/525-0200.** Cover $4 per person at tables; no cover at bar.

This is one of the most stylish jazz haunts in the Quarter. Nina and George Buck have created an oasis of civilized dining (linen on the table, lace curtains at the street windows, and international cuisine—see Chapter 5 for details) in which to present top-notch jazz groups Wednesday through Saturday. One very special feature is the collection of jazz records for sale in a back alcove, many of them real finds for the collector.

Praline Connection Gospel & Blues Hall. 901 South Peters St. ☎ **504/523-3973** for reservations and information.

You can't, and shouldn't, miss the Praline Connection's colorfully painted exterior. The 9,000-square-foot Praline Connection Gospel and Blues Hall offers live entertainment on Thursday, Friday, and Saturday nights. Every Sunday brings a great gospel brunch (served buffet style). Reservations are strongly recommended.

Preservation Hall. 726 St. Peter St. ☎ **504/523-8939.** Cover $3.

Dear to the hearts of all jazz devotees (and I count myself among them) is Preservation Hall, where jazz is found in its purest form, uncluttered by such refinements as air-conditioning, drinks, or even (unless you arrive very early) a place to sit. The shabby old building offers only hot, foot-tapping, body-swaying music, played by a solid core of old-time greats who never left New Orleans. Nobody seems to mind the lack of those other refinements—indeed, not only is the interior always packed, but its windows are frequently lined by the faces of those who stand on the sidewalk for hours just to listen.

Admission is unbelievably low, and if you want to sit on one of the much sought-after pillows right up front or a couple of rows of benches just behind them, be sure to get there a good 45 minutes before the doors open at 8pm. Otherwise, you must stand. The music goes on until 12:30am, with long sets interrupted by 10-minute breaks. The crowd continually changes as parents take children home at bedtime (the kids *love* the hall) and sidewalk listeners move in to take vacant places. There's a good collection of jazz tapes and CDs on sale.

Snug Harbor. 626 Frenchmen St. ☎ **504/949-0696.** Cover $8–$15, depending on performer.

On the fringes of the French Quarter (one block beyond Esplanade), Snug Harbor has earned top popularity from residents and visitors alike for its nightly presentation of contemporary jazz. Seating is on two levels to provide good viewing of the bandstand, and there's full dinner service featuring regional specialties as well as a light menu of sandwiches. The acts change every night. Shows are at 9 and 11pm nightly.

OUTSIDE THE FRENCH QUARTER

Bottom Line. 2101 N. Claiborne Ave. ☎ **504/947-9297.** Usually $5 cover.

Bottom Line attracts a youngish (25 and up) crowd and has three huge floors offering R&B and jazz. Saturday is ladies night.

Carrollton Station. 8140 Willow St. ☎ **504/865-9190.** $5–$15 cover.

This little nightclub not only has one of the best beer selections in New Orleans, but it also offers great live music Wednesdays through Sundays beginning at 10pm. Expect to hear anything and everything from acoustic blues to fusion jazz.

Lion's Den. 2655 Gravier St. ☎ **504/821-3745.**

The Lion's Den fills up unbelievably fast on Friday and Saturday nights when owner Irma Thomas performs. Call ahead for hours and prices.

Pampy's. 2005 N. Broad St. ☎ **504/949-7970.** Call for current cover charge.

Live jazz is offered in this tiny club Thursday through Sunday. It's a great little hole in the wall frequented mainly by locals.

Pete Fountain's. In the New Orleans Hilton, 2 Poydras St. ☎ **504/523-4374** or 504/561-0500. Cover varies; call for rates and to confirm show times.

Pete Fountain is one of those loyal native sons who has never been able to sever hometown ties. For more than 20 years he held forth in his own Bourbon Street club, but these days you'll find him here, in a re-creation of his former Quarter premises, which seats more than twice the number that could be accommodated in the old club. The plush interior—gold chairs and banquettes, red velvet bar chairs, lacy white iron-railinged gallery—sets the mood for the popular nightspot, located at the Mississippi River. Pete is featured in one show a night, Tuesday to Saturday at 10pm. You'll need reservations.

Tipitina's. 501 Napoleon Ave. ☎ **504/895-8477,** concert line 504/897-3943. Cover $4–$15 depending on the performer.

Here there's jazz, rhythm and blues, and almost every other form of music. At Tip's, it all depends on the artist playing, and that covers a *lot* of territory. Past performers in this New Orleans staple have included the Neville Brothers and Bo Diddley. Back in its 1977 beginnings this was home for the revered Professor Longhair until his death in 1980—it was named after one of his songs—and you'll be greeted by a bronze bust of the beloved musician as you enter. *Note:* As this book goes to press Tip's is for sale.

Vic's Kangaroo Cafe. 636 Tchoupitoulas St. ☎ **504/524-4329.**

As you might have guessed, the owner of this nightspot is a native of the land down under. In addition to serving meals, Vic's offers excellent blues music on Thursday from 10pm to 2am and on Saturday from 11pm to 3am. Vic's also has darts and a pool table located on the back patio (also known as the "Beer Garden").

2 Cajun & Zydeco

Maple Leaf Bar. 8316 Oak St. ☎ **504/866-9359.** Cover $3–$10, depending on day of week and performer.

Uptown in the Carrollton area, the Maple Leaf Bar may be the best place outside the bayous to hear Cajun music. Thursday nights and some weekends celebrate the lively music and dancing with standouts such as the Filé Cajun Band and the zydeco renditions of Dopsie and his Cajun Twisters. Other nights it might be rhythm and blues, rock and roll, or reggae. Dancing is "encouraged," so you may find yourself out on the floor two-stepping to that Cajun beat. Before the bands start at 10pm, there's a jukebox offering an eclectic mix of musical styles, from classical to jazz to ragtime to Cajun, and there's a strong tradition of good conversation ranging from literary subjects (poetry readings every Sunday afternoon feature local and visiting poets and writers) to music, sports, or almost any topic you choose.

Michaul's on St. Charles. 840 St. Charles Ave. ☎ **504/522-5517.** No cover.

You'll find good Cajun music here in the Warehouse District. If your feet begin tapping to the catchy rhythms but you're uncertain of the steps, Michaul's will give you free dance lessons. The cuisine is as Cajun as the music.

Mulate's. 201 Julia St. ☎ **504/522-1492.** No cover.

This Cajun restaurant, which has been popular in other parts of Louisiana, has recently opened in New Orleans. There's a huge central bar, and a stage for live Cajun music performances. Cajun dancing takes place nightly.

Patout's Cajun Cabin. 501 Bourbon St. ☎ **504/529-4256.** One-drink minimum.

Located right on Bourbon Street, Patout's Cajun Cabin features the music of Cajun Country as performed by The Can't Hardly Play Boys and Mudbug Deluxe. Drinks have equally odd names—try the Swamp Water. Music begins around 7pm every night.

3   Rock & the Rest of the Music Scene

IN THE FRENCH QUARTER & THE FAUBOURG MARIGNY

Cafe Brasil. 2100 Chartres St. ☎ **504/947-9386.** Cover varies according to performer.

Live music ranging from rock to Latin, Caribbean, and jazz is featured here nightly. The crowd is eclectic and multicultural, and the atmosphere is friendly and welcomes all lifestyles and varieties of people. Shows begin between 10 and 10:30pm every night.

Cafe Istanbul. 534 Frenchmen St. ☎ **504/944-4180.** Cover varies according to performer.

If your choices in music are varied, Cafe Istanbul (a Turkish restaurant by day) is just the place. You'll be able to hear anything from hip-hop to reggae to Latin music. Entertainment is live. Call ahead for the current schedule of events.

Cat's Meow. 701 Bourbon St. ☎ **504/523-1157.** No cover.

Cat's Meow is always full, and it's no wonder—they play popular rock songs all night long. The interior is bright and colorful, and the crowd the club attracts is young and loud. Karaoke is a favorite activity here, and you can even get a video tape of your performance.

Checkpoint Charlie's. 501 Esplanade Ave. ☎ **504/949-7012.** No cover.

There's live entertainment every night at Checkpoint Charlie's, and there's never a cover charge. Food and drink are plentiful, there are pool tables, and there's even a Laundromat and book exchange here. The fun never stops, whether you're doing laundry, playing video games, or kicking back at the bar, because Checkpoint Charlie is open 24 hours.

The Gold Mine. 701 Dauphine St. ☎ **504/586-0745.** Cover charge varies according to performer.

Famous for its "flaming Dr. Pepper" shooters (you have to see it to believe it), The Gold Mine keeps up with current trends in popular music. There are pool tables and a dance floor.

Howlin' Wolf. 828 St. Peter St. ☎ **504/523-2551.** $4–$8 cover charge.

Every night beginning around 10pm local college students gather here to listen to progressive rock bands.

Voodoo Groove. 216 Bourbon St. ☎ **504/523-2020.** $5 cover most nights.

If you've visited New Orleans before you'll recognize this place as the old Club Second Line. It's primarily a dance club, but if you're lucky you might arrive on a night when they're featuring an alternative rock band. Voodoo Groove is absolutely enormous.

OUTSIDE THE FRENCH QUARTER

Abstract Bookshop & Cafe. 1306 Magazine St. ☎ **504/522-2665.** Cover charge varies according to performer.

Located virtually under the highway overpass (I-10), the Abstract Bookshop and Cafe is one of the city's only genuine alternative rock/punk venues. Hours vary, so call ahead for details.

Amberjack's Down Under. 7306 Lake Shore Dr. ☎ **504/282-6660.** Cover on weekends only.

On most nights Amberjack's, which is located on the Lake Pontchartrain marina, is a favorite watering hole of local boaters. However, on Friday and Saturday nights singles hang out here listening to live classic rock and oldies while sipping tropical drinks. Pizzas and sandwiches are available.

Bart's on the Lake. 8000 Lake Shore Dr. ☎ **504/282-0271.** Cover on weekends only.

Offering exceptional views, pool tables, and video poker, Bart's on the Lake is a favorite of the 20- and 30-something crowd. It's located right next door to the New Canal Lighthouse, and on Friday and Saturday live entertainment is offered in the bar area, while on Sunday afternoon bands play on the dock. During the rest of the week a disc jockey keeps the place hopping.

City Lights. 310 Howard Ave. ☎ **504/568-1700.** $5 cover after 9pm.

City Lights is located in the Warehouse District, and as this book goes to press it is the most popular spot in New Orleans for the well-heeled 30-something crowd. Music runs the gamut from oldies to present-day Top 40.

Mid-City Lanes Rock & Bowl. 4133 S. Carrollton Ave. ☎ **504/482-3133.** Bowling day $8 per hour; evening rates Sun–Thurs $8 per hour, Fri–Sat $10 per hour. Admission to dance club is usually $5.

Another popular spot for some good ol' rock and roll is Mid-City Lanes Rock and Bowl. Yes, you guessed it, it's a rock club and a bowling alley—you literally rock *and* bowl. In 1995 Mid-City Lanes Rock and Bowl was named the best dance club by New Orleans Magazine. Mid-City opens around noon and stays open until everyone gets too tired to lift the ball.

4 The Bar Scene

It's sometimes hard to distinguish the bars from the music hot spots in New Orleans, but there are quite a few places you can go to relax and have a few drinks while shooting pool or playing a good game of foosball. There are also some upscale bars suitable for a business meeting or a quiet drink before or after dinner. In addition to the places listed below, most of the hotels have their own bars and lounges that are open to the general public.

IN THE FRENCH QUARTER & THE FAUBOURG MARIGNY

Apple Barrel. 609 Frenchmen St. ☎ **504/949-9399.**

If you're on your way up to Alberto's, an Italian restaurant located above the Apple Barrel (see Chapter 5 for a full listing), you might want to stop in here for a drink. Locals love this place and can often be found playing darts here.

Fashion Cafe. 619 Decatur St. ☎ **504/522-3181.**

If you just can't get enough of theme restaurants and bars, you won't be disappointed to find that the Fashion Cafe has just opened in New Orleans. Fashion memorabilia decorates all surfaces here, and there are two bars featuring oh-so-creatively named drinks like "The Catwalk" or "The Cover Girl." Fashion Cafe offers a full menu.

Hard Rock Cafe. 418 N. Peters St. ☎ **504/529-5617.**

Everyone knows what the Hard Rock Cafe is about by now. The focal point here is a guitar-shaped bar. A jukebox provides the music, and on Wednesdays you can get $1 longnecks.

Kerry Irish Pub. 331 Decatur St. ☎ **504/527-5954.** Call for cover charge.

First and foremost this place is a traditional Irish Pub; however, you can also hear live Irish and "alternative" folk music.

Lafitte's Blacksmith Shop. 941 Bourbon St. ☎ **504/523-0066.**

Lafitte's dates from 1772. Legend has it that the privateer brothers Pierre and Jean Lafitte used the smithy as a "blind" for their lucrative trade in contraband (and, some say, slaves they'd captured on the high seas). It had pretty much deteriorated by 1944, when a

Pat O'Brien & the Mighty Hurricane

Pat O'Brien's, 718 St. Peter St. (☎ **504/525-4823**), has been famous for as long as I can remember for its gigantic, rum-based Hurricane drink, served in 29-ounce hurricane lamp–style glasses. They may have outdone themselves now, though, with the three-gallon Magnum Hurricane. It's served with a handful of straws and takes a group to finish it—all of whom must drink standing up. Watch frat boys try this and drop one by one.

Pat O's let-your-hair-down conviviality has earned it a special place among so many residents that it sometimes has a neighborhood air usually associated with much smaller places—yes, locals drink here. There are three bars: the main bar at the entrance, a patio bar, and a large lounge located just off the entrance. The lounge is the center of a Pat O'Brien's entertainment. The fun comes from several teams of pianists alternating at twin pianos and an emcee who tells jokes. The entertainers seem to know every song ever written, and when they ask a patron, "Where're you from?" quick as a wink they'll break into a number associated with the visitor's home state. Requests are quickly honored, and sing-alongs develop all night long. There's no minimum and no cover, but if you buy a drink and it comes in a *glass* you'll be paying for the glass until you turn it in at the register for a $2 refund.

honeymooning visitor fell in love with it and devoted most of the rest of his life to making it a social center for artists, writers, entertainers, and journalists. He did this all without changing one iota of the musty old interior—even today you can see the original construction and "feel" what it must have been like when it was a privateers' hangout. Unfortunately Tom Caplinger's penchant for treating good friends such as Tennessee Williams and Lucius Beebe to refreshments "on the house" was stronger than his business acumen, and he eventually lost the building. All this is history, but I think it helps explain the comfortable, neighborhood air that still pervades Lafitte's. The interior is all exposed brick, wooden tables, and an air of authenticity. It's a good drop-in spot any time of day, but I especially enjoy relaxing in the dim, candlelit bar at the end of a festive night when "Miss Lily" Hood holds forth at the piano.

Napoleon House Bar & Cafe. 500 Chartres St. ☎ **504/524-9752.**

This landmark place is a favorite hangout of locals and tourists alike. Atmosphere is a big draw here. See Chapter 5 for a more complete listing.

O'Flaherty's Irish Channel Pub. 514 Toulouse St. ☎ **504/529-1317** or 504/529-4570.

The haunted courtyard in this 18th-century building is a big draw, but so is the Irish atmosphere. Irish dancing is offered every Saturday night.

Ol'Toone's Saloon. 233 Decatur St. ☎ **504/529-3422.**

It's not very atmospheric, but Ol'Toone's is a great place to go shoot pool and choose your tunes on the well-stocked jukebox.

Original Tropical Isle. 738 Toulouse St. ☎ **504/525-1689.**

If you're looking for a good, strong drink in a "tropical" setting, stop by the Original Tropical Isle and grab a "hand grenade." Other drinks have equally creative names—the "horny gator" is also very popular. Live music is featured here frequently.

Parrot's Perch. 721 Bourbon St., second floor. ☎ **504/529-4109.**

Margaritas and Corona and tequila shooters keep them coming back to Parrot's Perch every night. Sunday to Wednesday billiards are free.

Planet Hollywood. 620 Decatur St. ☎ **504/522-7826.**

Yes Virginia, there is a Planet Hollywood in New Orleans (they seem to be everywhere these days). Drinks are named for films and movie characters.

The "R" Bar. 1431 Royal St. ☎ **504/948-7499.**

The "R" Bar is the quintessential neighborhood bar. It attracts a varied clientele who come for the large selection of imported beers and the friendly, comfortable atmosphere.

Vino Vino. 1119 Decatur St. ☎ **504/529-4553.**

As its name suggests, Vino Vino is a wine bar—a huge step above the rest of the bars listed here. It's a great place for a pre- or post-dinner drink.

OUTSIDE THE FRENCH QUARTER
Audubon Tavern II. 6100 Magazine St. ☎ **504/895-9702.**

The clientele at Audubon Tavern II is mainly from neighboring college campuses. Dancing is virtually a requirement if you're going to stop here for a drink.

The Boot. 1039 Broadway Ave. ☎ **504/866-9008.**

Definitely a college bar (mainly due to its proximity to Tulane University), the atmosphere in The Boot is something like a frat party—Jell-O shooters being a favorite "libation." The drinks, as expected, are inexpensive, and specials are offered every day of the week.

Bruno's Bar. 7601 Maple St. ☎ **504/861-7615.**

For more than 60 years Bruno's has been a gathering place for fun-loving locals of all ages. Head for Bruno's for a few games of darts and a jukebox playing music spanning the last four decades.

The Bulldog. 3236 Magazine St. ☎ **504/891-1516.**

Yet another bar for the college crowd, The Bulldog has a fantastic selection of beers—currently more than 50 brews are offered. Video games and ear-splitting music make conversation difficult at best, but that's not why people hang at The Bulldog.

Hyttops Sports Bar. 500 Poydras Plaza (in the Hyatt Hotel). ☎ **504/561-1234.**

Sports fans take notice: Hyttops Sports Bar has seven big-screen TVs and no fewer than 11 smaller TVs all tuned, via satellite, to sporting events around the country. This is a great place to hang out after a Saints game.

Joe's Jungle Bar. 510 Gravier St. ☎ **504/524-9485.**

If you're in the Central Business District at quitting time, Joe's Jungle Bar will be jam packed with locals stopping for a drink on their way home from work. Nothing unusual here, just your regular bar drinks, a juke box, and video poker.

Madigan's. 800 S. Carrollton Ave. ☎ **504/866-9455.** No cover most nights.

Located in the Uptown section of New Orleans, Madigan's is a casual watering hole that's home to blues musician John Mooney on Sundays.

Nick's. 2400 Tulane Ave. ☎ **504/821-9128.**

The slogan here is "Looks like the oldest bar in town!" and it does. Behind the barroom you'll find billiards and infrequent performances by live musicians. Special drink prices are offered on weekdays.

Philips. 733 Cherokee St. ☎ **504/865-1155.**

Another favorite of the local university students, Philips offers good music and a number of video poker machines.

The Polo Lounge. 300 Gravier St. (in the Windsor Court Hotel). ☎ **504/523-6000.**

The Windsor Court is, without a doubt, the city's finest hostelry, and the Polo Lounge is the place to go if you're feeling particularly stylish. Sazeracs and cigars are popular here.

Saturn Bar. 3067 St. Claude Ave. ☎ **504/949-7532.**

The Saturn Bar has been around for almost 40 years, but it's only recently that celebrities like John Goodman and Nicolas Cage have made it famous. These days, it's the place to be for celebrity hounds. There's a good selection of imported beers available.

Sazerac Bar. In the Fairmont Hotel, University Place. ☎ **504/529-4733.**

Located in the posh Fairmont Hotel, Sazerac Bar is a favorite with the city's young professionals. The African walnut bar and murals by Paul Ninas complete the upscale atmosphere. The Sazerac Bar was featured in the movie *The Pelican Brief.* Wines and champagnes are available by the glass, and a dessert menu is available.

Sitting Duck. 5130 Freret St. ☎ **504/895-1400.**

All I can say is shots, shots, and more shots. The college crowd simply delights in the wide variety of shots offered here. The music is always very, very loud.

BREWHOUSES

These days brewhouses are popping up all over the country, and New Orleans is no exception. **Crescent City Brewhouse** (527 Decatur St., ☎ **504/522-0571**), primarily due to its central French Quarter location, is popular with tourists. The balcony, which faces Decatur Street, is always packed, and there are several original Crescent City beers on tap. A jazz combo plays here, and Happy Hour during the week brings two-for-one beer specials. There is a full menu.

Acadian Brewhouse, 201 N. Carollton Ave. (☎ **504/483-9003**), is a relative newcomer to the up-and-coming midcity area. All sorts of specialty beers, from Purple Haze to Blackened Voodoo are offered.

PIANO BARS

The Bombay Club. 830 Conti St. ☎ **504/522-5522** or 504/586-0972.

This posh piano bar features New Orleans jazz on Friday and Saturday evenings. Martinis at The Bombay Club are hailed as the best in town. Jeans and shorts are not acceptable attire.

Esplanade Lounge. In the Royal Orleans, 621 St. Louis St. ☎ **504/ 529-5333.**

For a nightcap to the strains of top-notch piano music in one of the city's loveliest settings, stop by the Esplanade.

A BAR WITH A VIEW

Top of the Mart. World Trade Center of New Orleans, 2 Canal St. ☎ **504/ 522-9795.**

The view is breathtaking any time of day, but especially so after dark, from the Top of the Mart, at the river. The world's largest revolving cocktail lounge located on the 33rd floor makes a complete circle about every 90 minutes. From up there you'll see the bend in the Mississippi that gives New Orleans its "Crescent City" title, and the reflected lights of ships in the harbor remind you that this is not only a fun town, but also a busy port. As you revolve, the layout of the city unfolds all the way to Lake Pontchartrain. There's no admission charge and no cover. Children aren't permitted. Top of the Mart is open daily until midnight or 1am.

5　Burlesque & Strip Clubs

As much a part of French Quarter lore as Mardi Gras and jazz are the legendary skin shows of Bourbon Street. There are a number of establishments offering this sort of entertainment in the 300 and 400 blocks of Bourbon; you'll be able to tell what you're getting into before you go in—club owners frequently open their doors to try to lure in the paying public with music and a more or less unobstructed view of the dancers inside. There is also a traditional cabaret theater in New Orleans; see below.

Chris Owens Club. 735 St. Louis St., corner of Bourbon St. ☎ **504/ 523-6400.** Cover $11 (includes show and one cocktail; $15 on New Year's Eve). Show times are Mon–Sat at 10pm and midnight.

If you like your entertainment on the sexy side but aren't quite game for Bourbon Street's strippers, this is the place to go. The talented and very beautiful Chris Owens, backed by a great group of musicians, puts on a show of fun-filled jazz, popular, country and western, and blues while (according to one devoted fan) revealing enough of her physical endowments to make strong men bay at the moon. Between shows, there's dancing on the elevated dance floor. Audience participation is encouraged—join in the conga line, which is popular with visitors and locals alike. Trumpeteer Al Hirt now performs at the Chris Owens Club several times a week. Hirt's shows usually begin at 8pm. Call to make reservations.

6 Gay Nightlife

Below you'll find listings of New Orleans's most popular gay nightspots. For more information you can check *Ambush,* which is a great source for the gay community in New Orleans and for those visiting. Ask around at some of the locally owned gay bars and restaurants and they'll tell you where to find the latest copy of *Ambush.*

BARS

In addition to those listed below, you might also try **Bus Stop,** 542 North Rampart St. (☎ **504/522-3372**), popular with the local African-American gay crowd; **The Golden Lantern,** 1239 Royal St. (☎ **504/529-2860**), a nice neighborhood spot where the bartender knows the clientele by name; and **Mrs. and Mr. B's on the Patio,** 515 St. Philip St. (☎ **504/586-0644**), popular with the local gay clientele for its beautiful patio (it's open 24 hours and has a happy hour from 4 to 9pm). If Levi's and leather is your scene, **The Rawhide,** 740 Burgundy St. (☎ **504/525-8106**), is your best bet; on Mardi Gras, this place hosts a great Gay Costume Contest that is not to be missed.

Bourbon Pub Parade. 801 Bourbon St. ☎ 504/529-2107.

The Bourbon Pub attracts a young male crowd, offering a video bar (with "dancing boys" on the weekend). Upstairs features a high-tech dance floor complete with lasers and smoke. Sunday nights bring a weekly T dance. It's open 24 hours and every time I've ever been in or been by, the place is packed.

Café Lafitte in Exile. 901 Bourbon St. ☎ 504/522-8397.

When Tom Caplinger lost Lafitte's Blacksmith Shop, friends say that it broke his heart. But he rallied and a little later opened a new place down the block toward Canal Street called the Café Lafitte in Exile (the exile is his own, from that beloved blacksmith shop). The new digs flourish as an elite gay bar even after his death. It is, in fact, the oldest gay bar in the country. There's a bar downstairs, and upstairs you'll find a pool table and a balcony that overlooks Bourbon Street.

Charlene's. 940 Elysian Fields. ☎ 504/945-9328.

Charlene's is known as the only lesbian bar in town. It's a little out of the way if you're staying in the Quarter, but there's dancing and live entertainment, so you might think it worth the trip. Take a cab.

Good Friends Bar & Queens Head Pub. 740 Dauphine St. ☎ 504/566-7199.

This is a good place to begin if it's your first visit to New Orleans. The local clientele is happy to offer suggestions as to where you might find the type of entertainment you're looking for. Downstairs there's a mahogany bar and a pool table. Upstairs is the quiet Queens Head Pub.

LeRoundup. 819 St. Louis St. ☎ **504/561-8340.**

LeRoundup attracts the most diverse crowd around. Here you'll find transsexuals lining up at the bar with drag queens and well-groomed men in khakis and Levi's. The atmosphere is friendly and very, very open, and in spite of the fact that it's only a half a block from the Bourbon Street scene, the clientele is primarily local. The bar is open 24 hours.

The Mint. 504 Esplanade Ave. ☎ **504/525-2000.** Cover charge varies according to performer.

A popular spot within the gay community in New Orleans, the Mint is always full. There's live entertainment all the time (including impersonation), so you should ask around or look in *Ambush* to find out what's happening during your visit. There's a very popular happy hour nightly from 5 to 9pm, and the club itself is open Monday through Friday from noon until the wee hours, Saturday and Sunday from 10am on.

DANCE CLUBS

Oz. 800 Bourbon St. ☎ **504/593-9491.**

One of New Orleans's newest dance clubs, at press time Oz was the place to see and be seen. It was ranked as the city's number-one dance club by *Gambit* magazine, and *Details* magazine ranked it as one of the top 50 clubs in the country. The music is great, there's an incredible laser light show, and from time to time there's a dancing-boys show atop the bar.

Rubyfruit Jungle. 640 Frenchmen St. ☎ **504/947-4000.**

The 80-foot copper-topped bar is enough of an attraction to make this place one of the city's hottest gay and lesbian dance clubs, but what everyone really comes for is the great music and high-tech lighting and sound. Each night brings a different kind of entertainment: Some nights offer New York warehouse-style dancing, others bring country and western, and still others feature comedy and other local gay talent.

Wolfendale's. 834 N. Rampart St. ☎ **504/523-7764.**

Popular with the city's gay African-American population, Wolfendale's has a lovely courtyard, a raised dance floor, and a pool table. Most don't come to lounge around in the courtyard or by the pool table. People come here to dance. Take a cab.

7 Gambling

So, you're probably wondering where you can go to gamble in New Orleans now that Harrah's highly touted casino has gone bust— before it even officially opened, I might add. Well, there's still a riverboat casino that remains in operation (see below), and if you're willing to make a short drive you can visit the **Boomtown Belle Casino,** located on the West Bank (call **504/366-7711** for information and directions), or the **Treasure Chest Casino,** docked on Lake Pontchartrain in Kenner (call **504/443-8000** for information and directions).

Flamingo Casino New Orleans. Riverwalk Marketplace, next to the New Orleans Hilton Riverside Hotel on Poydras Street at the river. ☎ **800/ 587-LUCK** or 504/587-5777. Admission $5. Call for cruise times or to see if the boat will be remaining dockside.

The *Flamingo* is an authentic re-creation of a 19th-century riverboat casino complete with authentic period detailing. There are 75 gaming tables and 1,333 slot machines. Table games include blackjack, craps, roulette, pai gow poker, and others. The boat actually cruises the Mississippi—it's not permanently docked, though there are times that it does remain docked, and at those times you're allowed unlimited boarding. Cruises last 90 minutes and take place about every three hours, beginning at 8:45am. I would strongly advise buying your tickets in advance, especially for the evening cruises, so you won't have to wait in line (lines can be enormously long), and getting there as soon as the doors open for boarding so you can stake out your machine before the masses beat you to it. Slot machines are the most popular form of gambling on the boat, and they range from 5¢ to $100 slots. At the time of my last visit, Lucky Dogs, Mother's, and the Italian restaurant Andrea's were the three food vendors represented. Drinks are free during your cruise, and there are smoke-free gaming rooms. Live Dixieland jazz is performed from time to time as well. Children are not allowed in the gaming rooms.

Index